D0561078

FUNERAL
SERVICES
FOR
TODAY

BY *James L. Christensen*
      Funeral Services
      The Minister's Service Handbook
      The Minister's Marriage Handbook
      The Complete Funeral Manual
      Contemporary Worship Services
      New Ways to Worship
      Creative Ways to Worship
      Funeral Services for Today

FUNERAL SERVICES FOR TODAY

James L. Christensen

FLEMING H. REVELL COMPANY

Old Tappan, New Jersey

Library of Congress Cataloging in Publication Data

Christensen, James L
    Funeral services for today.

    Includes bibliographical references.
    1. Funeral service. I. Title.
BV199.F8C52   265'.85   77-1350
ISBN 0-8007-0856-3

TO
my fellow ministers
who bear others' "burdens,
and so fulfil the law
[love] of Christ."

Galatians 6:2

CONTENTS

8 CONTENTS

1

FOR AN INFANT

Instrumental Prelude   "The King of Love My Shepherd Is"; "What a Friend We Have in Jesus"

The Opening Sentences   The eternal God is your dwelling place and underneath are the everlasting arms (Deuteronomy 33:27). Blessed are those who mourn, for they shall be comforted (Matthew 5:4). Blessed are the pure in heart, for they shall see God (Matthew 5:8, RSV).

Invocation Prayer   O God of Love, in whose protecting care our lives are eternally secure; our hope is ever in Thee. Quiet our troubled spirits, deep within our souls heal our grief. Thou hast the words of eternal life, so we rest our weary souls in Thee, through Jesus Christ our Lord. *Amen.*

Hymn (*optional*)   "Children of the Heavenly King" (*solo, song by congregation, organ interlude, or reading by minister*)

Scripture Readings
From the Old Testament   Lord, thou hast been our dwelling place in all generations. Before the mountains were brought forth, or ever thou hadst formed the earth and the world, from everlasting to everlasting thou art God (Psalms 90:1, 2).

The Lord is my shepherd, I shall not want; he makes me lie down in green pastures. He leads me beside still

9

waters; he restores my soul. He leads me in paths of righteousness for his name's sake. Even though I walk through the valley of the shadow of death, I fear no evil; for thou art with me; thy rod and thy staff, they comfort me. Thou preparest a table before me in the presence of my enemies; thou anointest my head with oil, my cup overflows. Surely goodness and mercy shall follow me all the days of my life; and I shall dwell in the house of the LORD for ever (Psalm 23).

He will feed his flock like a shepherd, he will gather the lambs in his arms, he will carry them in his bosom, and gently lead those that are with young (Isaiah 40:11).

From the New Testament   Some people brought children to Jesus for him to touch them, but the disciples scolded those people. When Jesus noticed it, he was angry and said to his disciples: "Let the children come to me! Do not stop them, because the Kingdom of God belongs to such as these. Remember this! Whoever does not receive the Kingdom of God like a child will never enter it." Then he took the children in his arms, placed his hands on each of them, and blessed them (Mark 10:13–16).

Let us give thanks to the God and Father of our Lord Jesus Christ, the merciful Father, the God from whom all help comes! He helps us in all our troubles, so that we are able to help those who have all kinds of troubles, using the same help that we ourselves have received from God. Just as we have a share in Christ's many sufferings, so also through Christ we share in his great help (2 Corinthians 1:3–5).

Poems (*optional*)

> And the mother gave, in tears and pain,
> The flowers she most did love;
> She knew she would see them again
> In the fields of light above.[1]

Baby Sleeps

> The baby wept;
> The mother took it from the nurse's arms,
> And hushed its fears, and soothed its vain alarms,
> And baby slept.

> Again it weeps;
> And God doth take it from the mother's arms,
> From present griefs, and future unknown harms,
> And baby sleeps.[2]

Pastoral Prayer God of all mercy, who art able to do abundantly more than we ask or think, who alone can heal the broken-in-heart; look tenderly upon these Thy children whose joy has been turned to sadness. We do not understand the untimely death of this child. We seek no answer to that which is a mystery to all. We ask only, O God, for greater faith in the promise that the light of Thy love is stronger than the darkness of death, and that in heaven little children behold Thy face. We are sustained, and the pain of separation is more bearable because we know Thou hast loved this child and will continue to love him through all eternity, in Thy heavenly home. Imprint this assurance deeply in our hearts this day.

Heavenly Father, as this sadness has drawn us closer to one another, renewing our love and our tenderness, so may it draw us closer to Thee. So may we not sorrow, as those who have no hope, but may we remember Jesus Christ risen from the dead, who said, "Because I live, you shall live also."

In the midst of our grief, renew our trusting, loving faith as we pray together as Jesus taught us: Our Father who art in heaven, hallowed be Thy name. Thy kingdom come, Thy will be done, on earth as it is in heaven. Give us this day our daily bread; and forgive us our debts, as we forgive our debtors; and lead us not into temptation, but deliver us from evil. For Thine is the Kingdom, and the Power, and the Glory forever. *Amen.*

Hymn (*optional*)   "He Shall Feed His Flock" (*solo or organ interlude*)

Meditation   "Of Such Is the Kingdom"

Today in our sorrow, we turn to the Bible, and in particular, the words of Jesus, for there is much information and comfort for the heavy heart.

"Let the children come to me," said Jesus, "for to such belongs the kingdom of God" (Mark 10:14).

There is no doubt in our minds about that, is there? Whatever else may be uncertain, our hearts affirm the statement: "Of such is the Kingdom of God."

We cannot think of anything more heavenly than an innocent, pure, trusting child. Is that not so?

We recognize something in a child that will never die. Jesus took "little ones in His arms and blessed them." It was as though He held an example of the eternal and heavenly in His arms. "Of such," He assured with confidence, "is the Kingdom of God."

One adult said, "What I would not give for the simple

innocence of childhood again." If heaven is composed of lives like this child's, then we can be comforted.

A Sunday-school teacher asked her class of ten-year-olds, "Where is heaven?" Quicker than a flash, one little girl spoke out, "Heaven is where Jesus is." No one could give a better answer.

It is not only where Jesus is, but where your little one and all children are who have died, for the one certainty to which we can cling is, "Of such is the Kingdom of God." Just this moment can you catch a glimpse of them both together? Jesus draws the child close to Himself, tenderly, lovingly, eternally.

Does not heaven come nearer now because his soul is there? If heaven is composed of children and Jesus Himself, and the Christlike, is not that comforting?

Does not his being there add one more attraction to heaven for you? Remember the qualifications: "Unless you . . . become like children [trusting, simple], you will never enter the kingdom of heaven." "Whoever humbles himself like this child, he is the greatest in the kingdom of heaven" (Matthew 18:3, 4).

Benediction This child, so precious to these parents, is equally dear to Thee, God of fatherly feelings. Enable them through the eyes of faith to know their child is safe and well and secure in the home where Thou art the eternal Father.

By Thy grace enable the parents to take up their lives again, blessed by the joy brought to them by this child, and ever looking forward to reunion with all they love through Jesus Christ, our Lord. *Amen.*

Postlude "I've Found a Friend, O Such a Friend"; "Lead Kindly Light"

Then he took the children in his arms.

2

FOR A SMALL CHILD

Instrumental Prelude   "Angel Voices, Ever Singing"; "Brightly Gleams Our Banner"

The Opening Sentences   "The LORD is near to all who call upon him, to all who call upon him in truth. He fulfils the desire of all who fear him, he also hears their cry, and saves them" (Psalms 145:18, 19).

Invocation Prayer   Almighty God, Lord of day and night, of the stormy sea and the quiet haven, of life and death: we turn to Thee. Hear our cry. Abide with us through the storms and troubles of this mortal life so that the clouds may lift, and the sea be calmed, and we may see the true home of our souls, through Jesus Christ our Lord. *Amen.*

Hymn (*optional*)   "Jesus, Saviour, Pilot Me" (*solo, song by congregation, organ interlude, or reading by minister*)

Scripture Readings
From the Old Testament   I lift up my eyes to the hills. From whence does my help come? My help comes from the LORD, who made heaven and earth. He will

not let your foot be moved, he who keeps you will not slumber. Behold, he who keeps Israel will neither slumber nor sleep.

The LORD is your keeper; the Lord is your shade on your right hand. The sun shall not smite you by day, nor the moon by night.

The LORD will keep you from all evil; he will keep your life. The LORD will keep your going out and your coming in from this time forth and for evermore (Psalm 121).

From the New Testament   At that moment the disciples came to Jesus, asking, "Who is the greatest in the Kingdom of heaven?" Jesus called a child, had him stand in front of them, and said: "Remember this! Unless you change and become like children, you will never enter the Kingdom of heaven. The greatest in the Kingdom of heaven is the one who humbles himself and becomes like this child. And the person who welcomes in my name one such child as this, welcomes me. . . . See that you don't despise any of these little ones. Their angels in heaven, I tell you, are always in the presence of my Father in heaven" (Matthew 18:1–5, 10).

"Do not be worried and upset," Jesus told them. "Believe in God, and believe also in me. There are many rooms in my Father's house, and I am going to prepare a place for you. I would not tell you this if it were not so. And after I go and prepare a place for you, I will come back and take you to myself, so that you will be where I am" (John 14:1–3).

This is how it will be when the dead are raised to life. When the body is buried it is mortal; when raised, it will be immortal. When buried, it is . . . weak; when raised, it will be beautiful and strong. When buried, it is a physical body; when raised it will be a spiritual body. There is, of course, a physical body, so there has to be a spiritual body (1 Corinthians 15:42–44).

Meditation   "The Amazing Future of Promise"

A baby in its prenatal days—if it could take voice— might say, "I don't want to be born. I am happy here. I am warm and protected." He might look at birth as we do death. But then he is born. He looks up into the kindest face he has ever known. He is cuddled, nourished, and protected, and grows in every human capacity.

Just so, death is a passing from this limited life into a new existence with amazing possibilities.

Just as some babies arrive prematurely, so this little life has made its entrance into the new world much too early from our perspective. It is painful to have him go so young. We are not ready. Great emotional sentiment surrounds his beautiful form. But we can be comforted in the biblical views about the future!

Paul wrote assuring that "if there is a physical body, there is also a spiritual body" (1 Corinthians 15:44).

These earthly bodies, however beautiful, are mortal. Yours is and so was your little son's. In the new world, he will have an imperishable body. Everything in this world changes, beauty fades and power diminishes, but in the life to come, lovely things will never cease to be lovely, and beautiful innocence will never lose its sheen.

In this earth, with its temptations and sins, young bodies, sooner or later, are dishonored by evil habits and uncontrollable passions. But in the life beyond, it is not so. With God's own finger, there is written on the breast—perfect purity, and on the brow—everlasting peace.

Our present bodies become weak and weary. How easily fatigued. We are limited in this existence with physical exhaustion. Our bodies require food, rest, sleep, medicine, healing. In the promised new life, no rough scars will ever stain the little hands; no earthly thorns shall ever wound the chubby round feet; no tears shall wet his eyelids; and no crying shall pass those serene lips. Nothing—no foreign element, no disease, no accident—can destroy the heavenly body.

Here, we have natural, physical limited bodies, imperfect vessels for the Spirit—imperfect instruments for God's use.

In the life to come, by happy contrast, God's Spirit can fill us and use us in ways not possible here. We will be able, as is your child now, to render perfect worship, perfect service, perfect love—and never grow tired.

"What I know now is only partial; then it will be complete, as complete as God's knowledge of me" (1 Corinthians 13:12 TEV). "What no eye has seen, nor ear heard, nor the heart of man conceived, what God has prepared for those who love him" (1 Corinthians 2:9).

What an exciting glorious new existence this must surely be for your son. We are assured of this by the Resurrection of our Lord who said, "Of such is the Kingdom of God."

Hymn (*optional*)   "Saviour, Like a Shepherd Lead Us" (*solo, song by congregation, organ interlude, or reading by minister*)

Benediction   Thanks be to God who gives us the victory through our Lord Jesus Christ! So then, my dear brothers, stand firm and steady. Keep busy always in your work for the Lord, since you know that nothing you do in the Lord's service is ever without value (1 Corinthians 15:57–58). *Amen.*

Postlude   "Around the Throne of God in Heaven"; "Open the Gates of the Temple"

"Your Father in heaven does not want any of these little ones to be lost."

3

FOR A BOY

Instrumental Prelude   "Jesus, Thou Joy of Loving Hearts"; "Jesus, the Very Thought of Thee"

The Opening Sentences   Cast your burden on the LORD, and he will sustain you . . . (Psalms 55:22). He heals the brokenhearted, and binds up their wounds (Psalms 147:3).

Invocation Prayer   Almighty and everlasting God, who is a very present help in trouble, our hearts are overwhelmed with grief. We turn to Thee, the Lord of all time, who was before the foundation of the world, and

will endure beyond this world of time, the same yesterday, today, and forever. May we in the experience of
Thy presence, find confidence; in the assurance of Thy
love, be lifted above our darkness; and in the Resurrection of Jesus, see a rainbow of promise and multicolored
dreams, forever and ever. *Amen.*

Hymn (*optional*) "Fairest Lord Jesus" (*solo, song
by congregation, organ interlude, or reading by minister*)

Scripture Readings
From the Old Testament The eternal God is your
dwelling place, and underneath are the everlasting
arms . . . (Deuteronomy 33:27).

As a father pities his children, so the LORD pities
those who fear him. For he knows our frame; he remembers that we are dust. As for man, his days are like
grass; he flourishes like a flower of the field; for the
wind passes over it, and it is gone, and its place knows
it no more. But the steadfast love of the LORD is from
everlasting to everlasting upon those who fear him, and
his righteousness to children's children, to those who
keep his covenant and remember to do his commandments (Psalms 103:13–18).

From the New Testament "See that you don't despise
any of these little ones. Their angels in heaven, I tell you,
are always in the presence of my Father in heaven. . . .
What do you think? What will a man do who has one
hundred sheep and one of them gets lost? He will leave
the other ninety-nine grazing on the hillside and go to
look for the lost sheep. When he finds it, I tell you, he
feels far happier over this one sheep than over the

ninety-nine that did not get lost. In just the same way your Father in heaven does not want any of these little ones to be lost" (Matthew 18:10; 12–14).

Soon afterward Jesus went to a town named Nain; his disciples and a large crowd went with him. Just as he arrived at the gate of the town, a funeral procession was coming out. The dead man was the only son of a woman who was a widow, and a large crowd from the city was with her. When the Lord saw her his heart was filled with pity for her and he said to her, "Don't cry." Then he walked over and touched the coffin, and the men carrying it stopped. Jesus said, "Young man! Get up, I tell you!" The dead man sat up and began to talk, and Jesus gave him back to his mother (Luke 7:11–15).

Pastoral Prayer   God, our Father, whose wisdom designed our existence, and whose goodness loved us into life—we thank Thee for the joy this child has brought to life. We thank Thee for all the good influences which have nurtured his development and those who surrounded him with love, and for the faith and tender care that brought forth the fruits of the Spirit.

Merciful Father, forgive our sins of omission, and our sins of commission.

Receive into Thy keeping and into Thine eternal love the soul of this child, dear to us, and dearer still to Thee.

May all our days be lived unto Thee, until the last morning breaks and the shadows flee away. Then, in Thy sweet mercy, unite us with those whom we have loved, we pray in the name of Jesus Christ, world without end. *Amen.*

Meditation "Taking Time to Smell the Roses"

There is a popular song, written in recent years, with the theme, "Stop, take time to smell the roses." We have come here to do just that.

Such a tragic experience as our friends have endured is a dark, foreboding happening, unless we can breathe deep from the garden of God's love and "smell the roses." There is much that is sad and ugly. Wise we would be to see the beautiful, and appreciate the few years of joy. Let the aroma of the roses permeate your being.

Many friends will be helpful to you in facing this loss. A family in Dodge City, Kansas, who lost their eight-year-old Scott can be especially comforting. They write:

> We would like to pass on a few words of gratitude to our many friends who helped us so much during our hour of tragedy. Our little Scott was taken away to heaven and we are perfectly happy in this, our only problem was trying to understand the timing and the reason. We have resigned ourselves to the fact that it was God's will and not ours to question.
>
> The faith we needed to endure our sorrow came from God through our many friends here on this earth. The response was overwhelming and so comforting. People can be so good in times of need, and we couldn't begin to relate all of the many acts of kindness without using this whole publication.
>
> Scotty touched so many more people in death than he ever could have in life and maybe helped us all to realize again that life itself is a very precious gift and one for which we should give thanks daily. In pondering the question of "Why would the Lord call an 8-year-old, who has his whole life ahead of him?" we

have to analyze what he really did have ahead of him. He had already walked barefooted in the grass, been taken to dream places known only to him by watching the clouds, smelled the flowers and marveled at their beauty, held a caterpillar in his hand (and probably in his pocket), seen the majestic Rockies and heard the mighty roll of thunder across the skies. He had indeed enjoyed some of the best things that God has provided for us on this earth. What Scotty had ahead of him was only things that would tend to engulf him as we all seem to be these days and all the beautiful things become commonplace and we take very little time to enjoy them. Stop and think about all the trials and temptations we face each week; we have very little time to embrace the wonderments of nature because some earthly schedule draws us by too quickly.

Let's not mourn the death of an 8-year-old; let's stop and smell the roses and maybe pass out a few to those of us who are still down here fighting out an existence. God bless you all and may we all be joined on the other shore to reap the really good things our Lord has in store.

THE FAMILY OF SCOTT DOWSE

Francis Greenwood Peabody felt this way also, for following the death of his son he wrote the immortal poem "Of Such Is the Kingdom":

My darling boy, so early snatched away
From arms still seeking thee in empty air,
That thou shouldst come to me I do not pray,
Lest, by thy coming, heaven should be less fair.

Stay, rather, in perennial flower of youth,
Such as the Master, looking on, must love;
And send to me the spirit of the truth,
To teach me of the wisdom from above.

Beckon to guide my thoughts, as stumblingly
They seek the kingdom of the undefiled;
And meet me at its gateway with thy key
The unstained spirit of a little child.[4]

Hymn (*optional*)   "My Faith Looks Up to Thee"
(*solo, song by congregation, organ interlude, or reading by minister*)

Benediction   May God, the source of hope, fill you
with all joy and peace by means of your faith in him,
so that your hope will continue to grow by the power
of the Holy Spirit (Romans 15:13), now and forever.
Amen.

Postlude   "Jesus, Lover of My Soul"; "Jerusalem, the
Golden"

*"Their angels in heaven are always in the
presence of my Father."*

4

FOR A GIRL

Instrumental Prelude   "In His Love Abiding, Wait on
the Lord"; "For the Beauty of the Earth"

The Opening Sentences   Comfort, comfort my people,
says your God. . . . "You are my servant, I have
chosen you and not cast you off"; fear not, for I am

with you, be not dismayed, for I am your God; I will strengthen you, I will help you, I will uphold you with my victorious right hand (Isaiah 40:1; 41:9, 10).

Invocation Prayer Father of mercy, Giver of all comfort, grant that during these moments of memorial and coronation in Thy presence those upon whom this death so closely falls may find the consolation of Thy love, the support of caring friends, the promise of eternal life in Thy Kingdom, and the bright light of faith and hope through Jesus Christ who brought life and immortality to light. *Amen.*

Hymn (*optional*) "Come, Ye Disconsolate" (*solo, song by congregation, organ interlude, or reading by minister*)

Scripture Readings
From the Old Testament The LORD is my light and my salvation; whom shall I fear? The LORD is the stronghold of my life; of whom shall I be afraid? . . . Though a host encamp against me, my heart shall not fear; though war arise against me, yet I will be confident. One thing have I asked of the LORD, that will I seek after; that I may dwell in the house of the LORD all the days of my life, to behold the beauty of the LORD, and to inquire in his temple. For he will hide me in his shelter in the day of trouble; he will conceal me under the cover of his tent, he will set me high upon a rock. And now my head shall be lifted up above my enemies round about me; and I will offer in his tent sacrifices with shouts of joy; I will sing and make melody to the LORD. Hear, O LORD, when I cry aloud, be gracious to me and answer me! Thou hast said, "Seek

ye my face." My heart says to thee, "Thy face, LORD,
do I seek." Hide not thy face from me. . . .

I believe that I shall see the goodness of the LORD in
the land of the living! Wait for the LORD; be strong and
let your heart take courage; yea, wait for the LORD!
(Psalms 27:1; 3–9; 13, 14).

God is our refuge and strength, a very present help
in trouble. Therefore we will not fear though the earth
should change, though the mountains shake in the heart
of the sea; though its waters roar and foam, though the
mountains tremble with its tumult. There is a river
whose streams make glad the city of God, the holy habitation of the Most High (Psalms 46:1–4).

From the New Testament Jesus went back across to
the other side of the lake. There at the lakeside a large
crowd gathered around him. Jairus, an official of the
local synagogue, came up, and when he saw Jesus he
threw himself down at his feet and begged him as hard
as he could: "My little daughter is very sick. Please
come and place your hands on her, so that she will get
well and live!" Then Jesus started off with him. . . .
some messengers came from Jairus' house and told him,
"Your daughter has died. Why should you bother the
Teacher any longer?" Jesus paid no attention to what
they said, but told him, "Don't be afraid, only believe."
Then he did not let anyone go on with him except Peter
and James and his brother John. They arrived at the
official's house, where Jesus saw the confusion and
heard all the loud crying and wailing. He went in and
said to them, "Why all this confusion? Why are you
crying? The child is not dead—she is only sleeping!"
They all started making fun of him, so he put them all

out, took the child's father and mother, and his three disciples, and went into the room where the child was lying. He took her by the hand and said to her, *Talitha koum,* which means, "Little girl! Get up, I tell you!" She got up at once and started walking around . . . (Mark 5:21–24, 35–42).

Meditation   "Life after Life"

Numbed, heartbroken, disenchanted, we come here. In these moments together we want to thank God for the joy this little girl has brought to our lives. We want to share with the family the loss, and convey to them our love, and to promise our sustaining support as they assimilate this death into their life. When other helpers fail and comforts flee, we turn to God. We want to reaffirm our faith in the reality of the unseen, in the love of our Heavenly Father, and the future home provided for God's children.

It was the mission of Jesus to comfort the sorrowing. "He has sent me," He said, "to bind up the brokenhearted." The church which He established continues His work of love. It is her mission to sound the note of comfort in fulfillment of the psalmist's prayer, "The LORD answer you in the day of trouble!" (Psalms 20:1).

Jesus' deathless words bring comfort in the hour of earth's supreme anguish: "Come to me, all who labor and are heavy laden, and I will give you rest. Take my yoke upon you, and learn from me; for I am gentle and lowly in heart, and you will find rest for your souls. For my yoke is easy, and my burden is light" (Matthew 11:28–30).

"I came that they may have life, and have it abundantly" (John 10:10).

"I am the resurrection and the life; he who believes in me, though he die, yet shall he live, and whoever lives and believes in me shall never die. Do you believe this?" (John 11:25, 26).

"Let not your hearts be troubled; believe in God, believe also in me. In my Father's house are many rooms; if it were not so, would I have told you that I go to prepare a place for you? And when I go and prepare a place for you, I will come again and will take you to myself, that where I am you may be also" (John 14:1–3).

There is also comfort from others whose faith has sustained them. Their poems reveal their feelings.

Poems (*optional*)

Childhood

Thy days, my darling one, were few—
    An angel's morning visit,
That came and vanished with the dew—
    'Twas here—'tis gone—where is it?

I cannot tell to what sweet dell
    The angels may have borne thee;
But this I know, thou canst not go
    Where my heart will fail to find thee.[5]

There Is No Death

There is no death! The stars go down
To rise upon some other shore,
And bright in heaven's jeweled crown
They shine for evermore.

There is no death! An angel form
Walks o'er the earth with silent tread;

He bears our best loved things away,
And then we call them "dead."

He leaves our hearts all desolate;
He plucks our fairest, sweetest flowers;
Transplanted into bliss, they now
Adorn immortal bowers.[6]

Gone to School

She is not dead—the child of our affection—
But gone unto that school
Where she no longer needs our poor protection,
And Christ Himself doth rule.

In that great cloister's stillness and seclusion,
By guardian angels led,
Safe from temptation, safe from sin's pollution,
She lives, whom we call dead.

Day after day we think what she is doing
In those bright realms of air;
Year after year, her tender steps pursuing,
Behold her grown more fair.

Thus do we walk with her and keep unbroken
The bond which nature gives,
Thinking that our remembrance, though unspoken,
May reach her where she lives.[7]

Pastoral Prayer Our Heavenly Father, who does love us with an everlasting love; we thank Thee for the eternal home of light and joy and love where little children play and sing, and with unstained hearts grow in stature and beauty amid scenes of peace.

We thank Thee for the gift of Thy love, loaned to these friends for a while, to be for them now a sacred and joyful memory. Lift their thoughts beyond their sadness to Thy presence and the eternal abode where the child of their love awaits their heavenly homecoming. May the memory sustain their hope and love of Thee, and help them live in the light of eternity.

Amid our earthly trials, dear Father, keep within us all the spirit of little children, knowing the favor of the Lord. May we strive to remove from the world all things that would injure Thy children, inspired by that Babe who came into the world, then grew in wisdom and stature and in favor with Thee and men, even Jesus Christ, our Lord. *Amen.*

Hymn (*optional*) "O Love That Wilt Not Let Me Go" (*solo, song by congregation, organ interlude, or reading by minister*)

Benediction The grace of our Lord Jesus Christ, the love of God, and the communion of the Holy Spirit be with us all to the end, and in the end. *Amen.*

Postlude "Safe in the Arms of Jesus"; "Guide Me, O Thou Great Jehovah"

Instead, it was a better country they longed for.

5

FOR A TEENAGE YOUTH

Instrumental Prelude "Prelude in E Minor" (Chopin); "Saviour, Thy Dying Love"

The Opening Sentences   They who wait for the Lord shall renew their strength, they shall mount up with wings like eagles, they shall run and not be weary, they shall walk and not faint (Isaiah 40:31).

For the mountains may depart and the hills be removed, but my steadfast love shall not depart from you, and my covenant of peace shall not be removed, says the Lord, who has compassion on you (Isaiah 54:10).

Invocation Prayer   O Thou who art from everlasting to everlasting, we turn to Thee in faith wherein is our hope in the experience of death. Comfort with love and hope these upon whom this loss is so intimately felt, so they may turn their thoughts from that which is lost to that which can never be lost, through Thy promises in Jesus Christ our Lord. *Amen.*

Scripture Readings
From the Old Testament   God is our refuge and strength, a very present help in trouble. Therefore we will not fear though the earth should change, though the mountains shake in the heart of the sea; though its waters roar and foam, though the mountains tremble with its tumult. . . . "Be still, and know that I am God. I am exalted among the nations, I am exalted in the earth!" The Lord of hosts is with us; the God of Jacob is our refuge (Psalms 46:1–3; 10, 11).

Bless the Lord, O my soul; and all that is within me, bless his holy name! Bless the Lord, O my soul, and forget not all his benefits. . . . For as the heavens are high above the earth, so great is his steadfast love toward those who fear him; as far as the east is from the west, so far does he remove our transgressions from us. As a father pities his children, so the Lord pities those who fear him. For he knows our frame; he remembers that we are dust. As for man, his days are like grass; he flourishes like a flower of the field; for the wind passes over it, and it is gone, and its place knows it no more. But the steadfast love of the LORD is from everlasting to everlasting upon those who fear him, and his righteousness to children's children, to those who keep his covenant and remember to do his commandments (Psalms 103:1, 2; 11–18).

From the New Testament

"Come to me, all of you who are tired from carrying your heavy loads, and I will give you rest. Take my yoke and put it on you, and learn from me, for I am gentle and humble in spirit; and you will find rest. The yoke I will give you is easy, and the load I will put on you is light" (Matthew 11:28–30).

"I have come in order that they might have life, life in all its fulness" (John 10:10).

"In a little while the world will see me no more, but you will see me; and because I live, you also will live" (John 14:19).

Jesus said to her: "I am the resurrection and the life. Whoever believes in me will live, even though he dies; and whoever lives and believes in me will never die . . ." (John 11:25, 26).

Instead, it was a better country they longed for, the heavenly country. And so God is not ashamed to have them call him their God, for he has prepared a city for them (Hebrews 11:16).

Poem (*optional*)

This I Know

Only for a little space
Songs of joy are still—
Only through a midnight's watch
Shall our tears be spilled.

Only for a little while
Cloud-banks will be dark,
Then will fingers, quite unseen,
Paint the rainbow's arc.

This I know, though gleaming threads
Of our lives be crossed,
Yet a space and we shall find
Songs we thought were lost.[8]

Pastoral Prayer   Merciful God and Father, we thank
Thee for this young life, which we memorialize today,
rich in intelligence, ambition, good humor, and unselfishness. May the memories of his radiant charm dispel
the spirit of heaviness.

Help us, Eternal Spirit, to know that a successful life
is not in its duration but in its inspiration; not in number of years but in its character and service. We remember that Jesus was young when He died upon the cross,
yet His influence was expanded in death, assuring, "Because I live, you too shall live!"

O Lord, with Your Spirit growing within us, we
choose this moment to become gentle, more compassionate, more loving, more caring, more Christlike per-
sons, thus to live out Thy will and to become more
assured of heaven's rewards, in Jesus' name. *Amen.*

Hymn (*optional*)   " 'Are Ye Able,' Said the Master" (*solo, song by congregation, organ interlude, or reading by minister*)

Meditation   "Life Beyond Life"

When George Papashvily, one of the authors of *Anything Can Happen,* was a small boy, he was taken to see a revered old man who lived alone. It was customary for each child to give the hermit a gift, and receive in return a special proverb.

The old man was stern, with a long white beard. George was frightened as he went. The old man beckoned him to come close. They talked. Presently the man said, "Son, I am going to give you your proverb, something to help when you are sad or tired or discouraged; something to remember when you doubt and fear."

The old man bent down and whispered in his ear, "This moment, too, is part of eternity."

Even the most fleeting moments are a part of eternity. Eternity begins here. Birth and death are not two irreconcilable parts, they form a harmonious whole. Death is not an event left out of the Creator's scheme for humans. Like birth, death comes to every person sooner or later—to some sooner than anticipated. To many, death comes in the springtime of life.

In this world we see only a small part of the whole of life. Like an iceberg, only a small segment appears— all the rest is unseen. The great majority of the earth's population still die in youth and childhood.

John Keats, the poet with an eternal love for beauty, died at the age of twenty-six. There is no meaning at all to personality or anything for that matter, unless there is continuation of the life framed here. All education, all striving, all development is in vain if death ends all.

We dare to believe "this moment, too, is part of eternity." Perhaps _____'s greatest work was already accomplished. Some do more good in a few short years filled with a quality of faith and dedication than others accomplish in five times more years, for

> We live in deeds, not years; in thoughts, not breath;
> In feelings, not figures on a dial.
> We should count time by heart-throbs when they beat,
> For God, for man, for duty. He most lives,
> Who thinks most, feels the noblest, acts the best.
> Life is but a means unto an end—that end,
> Beginning, mean, and end to all things—God.[9]

Who can measure the posthumous influence of Joan of Arc who was burned alive in her youth, and whose life has influenced the best minds and lives of ages since. Who can estimate the power of Edith Cavell's martyrdom, whose last words were, "I must have no hatred nor bitterness toward anyone." The military chaplain who conducted her funeral could not contain his admiration, and attested, "She was courageous to the end. She professed her Christian faith and said that she was glad to die for her country. She died like a heroine."

The supreme example, of course, is Jesus Christ who was killed while relatively young. But God used His life and His death to jar the calloused conscience of men and to draw them to the new life. He accomplished God's mission for His life by dying. Our dear young friend has accomplished much even in dying. We thank God for his life, though it was brief. "This moment, too, belongs to eternity."

Hymn (*optional*) "God, Who Touchest Earth with Beauty" (*solo, song by congregation, organ interlude, or reading by minister*)

Benediction May the God who gives us peace make you completely his, and keep your whole being, spirit, soul, and body, free from all fault, at the coming of our Lord Jesus Christ (1 Thessalonians 5:23). *Amen.*

Postlude "I Know That My Redeemer Lives" (Handel)

The Lord is merciful and gracious.

6

FOR A DRUG VICTIM

Instrumental Prelude   "Rock of Ages"; "Sun of My Soul"

The Opening Sentences The LORD is merciful and gracious . . . . He does not deal with us according to our sins, nor requite us according to our iniquities. For as the heavens are high above the earth, so great is his steadfast love toward those who fear him . . . . As a father pities his children, so the LORD pities those who fear him (Psalms 103:8–13).

Invocation Prayer Thanks be to Thee, O God, for when we turn to Thee, we find Thou hast already turned to us. Thanks be to Thee, O God, for when we remember Jesus Christ, the best within us is awakened, and we are drawn to Thee. Thanks be to Thee, O God, for when we are in the presence of death, we are quieted for we know there is more to life. In this worship service, speak to us of eternal matters, and quiet our spirits with forgiving love, that we may hear and believe, and live more nobly, in the light of Jesus Christ. *Amen.*

Scripture Readings

From the Old Testament O LORD, our Lord, how majestic is thy name in all the earth! Thou whose glory above the heavens is chanted by the mouth of babes and infants, thou hast founded a bulwark because of thy foes, to still the enemy and the avenger. When I look at thy heavens, the work of thy fingers, the moon and the stars which thou hast established; what is man that thou art mindful of him, and the son of man that thou dost care for him? Yet thou hast made him little less than God, and dost crown him with glory and honor. Thou hast given him dominion over the works of thy hands; thou hast put all things under his feet, all sheep and oxen, and also the beasts of the field, the birds of the air, and the fish of the sea, whatever passes along the paths of the sea. O LORD, our Lord, how majestic is thy name in all the earth! (Psalm 8).

From the New Testament In the past you were spiritually dead because of your disobedience and sins. At that time you followed the world's evil way; you obeyed the ruler of the spiritual powers in space, the spirit who now controls the people who disobey God. Actually all of us were like them, and lived according to our natural desires, and did whatever suited the wishes of our own bodies and minds. Like everyone else, we too were naturally bound to suffer God's wrath.

But God's mercy is so abundant, and his love for us is so great, that while we were spiritually dead in our disobedience he brought us to life with Christ; it is by God's grace that you have been saved. In our union with Christ Jesus he raised us up with him to rule with him in the heavenly world. He did this to demonstrate for all time to come the abundant riches of his grace in the love he showed us in Christ Jesus. For it is by God's grace that you have been saved, through faith. It is not your own doing, but God's gift. There is nothing here to boast of, since it is not the result of your own efforts. God is our Maker, and in our union with Christ Jesus he has created us for a life of good works, which he has already prepared for us to do (Ephesians 2:1–10).

But do not forget this one thing, my dear friends! There is no difference in the Lord's sight between one day and a thousand years; to him the two are the same. The Lord is not slow to do what he has promised, as some think. Instead, he is patient with you, because he does not want anyone to be destroyed, but wants all to turn away from their sins.

But the Day of the Lord will come as a thief. On that Day the heavens will disappear with a shrill noise, the heavenly bodies will burn up and be destroyed, and the earth with everything in it will vanish. Since all these things will be destroyed in this way, what kind of people should you be? Your lives should be holy and dedicated to God, as you wait for the Day of God, and do your best to make it come soon—the Day when the heavens will burn up and be destroyed, and the heavenly bodies will be melted by the heat. But God has promised new heavens and a new earth, where righteousness will be at home, and we wait for these.

And so, my friends, as you wait for that Day, do your best to be pure and faultless in God's sight and to be at peace with him. Look on our Lord's patience as the opportunity he gives you to be saved . . . . But continue to grow in the grace and knowledge of our Lord and Savior Jesus Christ. To him be the glory, now and for ever! Amen (2 Peter 3:8–18).

Pastoral Prayer   God and Father of our spirits, who has been speaking to us through the Holy Scriptures, and in the words of Thy Son, Jesus Christ, grant that our minds and hearts may be receptive to Thy Truth, and that we may learn those things that belong to peace.

We have gathered before Thee, O God, as those who shared this life, but whose face we behold no more. In the silence, we recount with thanksgiving his friendship and endearing qualities.

O God of mercy and compassion, forgive us all, for we have fallen short of Thy will. We have turned to our own ways, betrayed our highest ideals, neglected our noblest opportunities, provided a poor example, and brought grief to Thee and others. O God, unto whom all hearts are open, forgive our past. Comfort us with the words of Jesus, "[Whoever] comes to me I will not cast out" (John 6:37). Set our feet on new paths to obey, love, and serve Thee.

Father, to every life that is saddened, be that soul's comfort and hope. To every heart that is weary and torn, be its rest and renewal. Where family ties or friendships have been broken, may there be a new awareness that we all belong to one another because we all belong to Thee.

Grant us grace, now to commit the spirit into Thy strong keeping, in whom alone is everlasting life, and peace of soul, through Jesus Christ. *Amen.*

Hymn (*optional*)   "There's a Wideness in God's Mercy" (*solo, song by congregation, organ interlude, or reading by minister*)

Meditation   "Comfort in God's Love"

Ringing in my mind is the song "Everybody Loves Somebody, Some Time." On this occasion we are met here because "everybody here loved this person, _____, some time." He was loved by his family, but above all he was loved by God, his Heavenly Father.

The Bible in many different stories tells of God's love —by the shepherd who hunted all over the mountain range for a lost sheep that had wandered from the fold; by the woman hunting all through the house for a carelessly handled coin that had been kicked and rolled out of circulation; by the rebellious boy who violated all the family trust and broke his parents' hearts, then finally returned and was received joyously by his dad. Each illustrate the way of God's love. At the heart of existence is love, God's love for each of us.

It is not my purpose here to eulogize our friend nor pronounce ecclesiastical judgment. Such is the prerogative of God who alone determines the destiny of our lives. So, let us think about God.

The starting point—the center and core of all things —is God. No man designed human life or the universe. There is One behind all that we see and all that we do not. "In the beginning God" reads the Bible. God placed us in this world and prepared it as our home, even before we comprehended Him—even before we were perceptive enough to know Him—even when we are unconscious of Him—even when we live as if He did not.

God cannot be seen, nor can He be put into a test tube. In this scientific age some think we must prove everything by isolating it as an object. Because they have never seen God as a "giant somewhere in the sky," they conclude there is no God. They say, "Here is a book; there is a tree; yonder is a car; where is God?" God is not an object. God is not an *it*. God is a *Thou;* not a *what* but a *who*. He is Spirit. He is the *person* in personality. He is the *conscious* in consciousness. He is the *ground of being* from which being blossoms. God is not in the world: the world is in God.

The late Dr. Toyohiko Kagawa, famous Japanese Christian leader and teacher, used to say our relationship with God was analogous to an unborn baby's relationship with its mother. The child in its mother's womb cannot see its mother's face, or hear her speak in audible ways. It can only feel the wall of the abdomen. Its world is terribly limited. If the baby could take voice, it might say, "There is no mother," all the while it is surrounded by its mother. Many people are that way about God. They see the wall, but no one with whom the wall is associated. The world is the clothing of God, in which we see His beauty, order, and purpose. Or, if you like, the world is the inside of God's uni-body. Death is being born into the outside where we can hear, understand, and know Him better.

Meanwhile, Jesus Christ is a brother, born of human flesh, as are we, to show us while here in this confinement the love of God—and that is good news! Indeed it is!

One night a friend questioned Peter Marshall about whether he really thought we shall ever have to stand before God on a Judgment Day and hear the roll call of our sins.

"Yes, the Bible makes it quite clear," Peter answered promptly. "Someday, somewhere, somehow, there will be an accounting for each of us."

He paused and seemed lost in thought as he stirred his third cup of tea. "I think I may have to go through the agony of hearing all my sins recited in the presence of God. But I believe it will be like this—Jesus will come over and lay His hand across my shoulders and say to God, 'Yes, all these things are true, but I'm here to cover up for Peter. He is sorry for all his sins, and by a transaction made between us, I am now solely responsible for them.' " [10]

With a brother like that as Savior, who reveals to us a God with a love like that, let us lift up our heads, put a smile on our faces, and begin the task of getting to know God better—now, before being ushered into the mysterious unknown.

Benediction Now may the love of God as conceived and experienced in Jesus Christ, give you peace, renewal, and a new lease upon life, now and forever. *Amen.*

Postlude "Jesus, Lover of My Soul"; "O Love That Wilt Not Let Me Go"

I have done my best in the race, I have run the full distance.

7

FOR A MILITARY YOUTH

Instrumental Prelude "I Bind My Heart This Tide"; "We Would Be Building" (*Finlandia*)

The Opening Sentences I have done my best in the race, I have run the full distance, I have kept the faith. And now the prize of victory is waiting for me, the crown of righteousness which the Lord, the righteous Judge, will give me on that Day—and not only to me, but to all those who wait with love for him to appear (2 Timothy 4:7, 8).

Invocation Prayer O God, O Lord, what a Friend You have been. When we have been lonely, You have encouraged us. When serving, You have supported us. When struggling, You have strengthened us. Now in our deep distress, as we pass under the shadow of great affliction, lonely in bereavement—O Lord, Intimate Friend, comfort us with Your presence. Fill our desolate hearts with peace and with pride, so that we may cling closely to Thee, who art able to turn shadows of night into morning light through Jesus Christ and His Resurrection. *Amen.*

Scripture Readings

From the Old Testament The LORD is my light and my salvation; whom shall I fear? The LORD is the stronghold of my life; of whom shall I be afraid? . . . Though a host encamp against me, my heart shall not fear; though war arise against me, yet I will be confident. One thing have I asked of the LORD, that will I seek after; that I may dwell in the house of the Lord all the days of my life, to behold the beauty of the LORD, and to inquire in his temple. For he will hide me in his shelter in the day of trouble; he will conceal me under the cover of his tent, he will set me high upon a rock. . . . I believe that I shall see the goodness of the LORD in the land of the living! Wait for the LORD; be strong, and let your heart take courage; yea, wait for the LORD! (Psalms 27:1; 3–6; 13; 14).

From the New Testament "Do not be worried and upset," Jesus told them. "Believe in God, and believe also in me. There are many rooms in my Father's house, and I am going to prepare a place for you. I would not tell you this if it were not so. And after I go and prepare a place for you, I will come back and take you to myself, so that you will be where I am. . . . I will not leave you alone; I will come back to you. In a little while the world will see me no more, but you will see me; and because I live, you also will live. . . . Whoever loves me will obey my message. My Father will love him, and my Father and I will come to him and live with him. Whoever does not love me does not obey my words. The message you have heard is not mine, but comes from the Father who sent me. I have told you this while I am still with you. The Helper, the Holy Spirit whom the Father will send in my name, will teach you everything, and make you remember all that I have told you. Peace I leave with you; my own peace I give you. I do not give it to you as the world does. Do not be worried and upset; do not be afraid" (John 14:1–3; 18–19; 23–27).

There is no condemnation now for those who live in union with Christ Jesus. . . . Whoever does not have the Spirit of Christ does not belong to him. But if Christ lives in you, although your body is dead because of sin, yet the Spirit is life for you because you have been put right with God. If the Spirit of God, who raised Jesus from death, lives in you, then he who raised Christ from death will also give life to your mortal bodies by the presence of his Spirit in you. . . . God's Spirit joins himself to our spirits to declare that we are God's children. Since we are his children, we will possess the blessings he keeps for his people, and we will also possess with Christ what God has kept for him; for if we share Christ's suffering, we will also share his glory. I consider that what we suffer at this present time cannot be compared at all with the glory that is going to be revealed to us. . . . For we know that in all things God works for good with those who love him, those whom he has called according to his purpose. . . . Faced with all this, what can we say? If God is for us, who can be against us? He did not even keep back his own Son, but offered him for us all! He gave us his Son —will he not also freely give us all things? . . . Who, then, can separate us from the love of Christ? Can trouble do it, or hardship, or persecution, or hunger, or poverty, or danger, or death? . . . No, in all these things we have complete victory through him who loved us! For I am certain that nothing can separate us from his love: neither death nor life; neither angels nor other heavenly rulers or powers; neither the present nor the future; neither the world above nor the world below— there is nothing in all creation that will ever be able to separate us from the love of God which is ours through Christ Jesus our Lord (Romans 8:1; 9–11; 16–18; 28; 31, 32; 35; 37–39).

Pastoral Prayer   Thank you, Heavenly Father, for the eternal perspective to life. It is not how long we live that counts; it is how meaningfully we live that matters. It is the donation of the life more than duration that adds eternal significance to a life.

We thank You, dear God, for the cherished memories that will forever enrich our lives because of _____, who gave himself in unselfish dedication for mankind's freedom, and who has been taken to live and love with You.

From the inspiration of his life, and the beautiful example of Jesus, our Lord, help us to make our lives more dedicated, more devoted, more unselfish, that we may through beautiful living justify in fruitful and creative work, the longer years You are giving us.

Set before us the figure of Jesus with His work. It seemed unfinished and His life premature and tragically cut short by death on the cross; yet in the timelessness of His integrity, He fulfilled life and lives forever. Let us hear His helpful words, "Peace I leave with you; my peace I give unto you. . . . I have finished the work which was given me to do . . . Let not your hearts be troubled." So may it be. *Amen.*

Hymn (*optional*)   "Now in the Days of Youth" (*solo, song by congregation, organ interlude, or reading by minister*)

Meditation   "Why Must My Son Die?"

The Oakland Raider football team has its training camp in Santa Rosa, California. In close proximity is the Jack London State Historical Park, which is a memorial to the turn-of-the-century author of *The Sea Wolf, The Call of the Wild,* and *White Fang.*

A newspaper reporter returning to the camp read quarterback Kenny Stabler a sample of London's prose.

> I would rather be ashes than dust! I would rather that my spark should burn out in a brilliant blaze than it should be stifled by dryrot.
>
> I would rather be a superb meteor, every atom in me in magnificent glow, than a sleepy and permanent planet. The proper function of man is to live, not to exist. I shall not waste my days in trying to prolong them. I shall use my time."

"What does that mean to you, Stabler?" asked the sportswriter.

"Throw deep," Stabler said.[11]

We are met here to honor a young man who lived life to its fullest, every atom aglow. He was more interested in quality of life than in quantity of years. He "threw deep."

It is most fitting that we have come here to convey sympathy and love to our dear friends in the death of their son. In a true sense, it is a mutual loss to the family, to this community, and to our nation for whose defense he laid down his life. All of us mourn his death.

It is utterly appropriate that we express corporately what we personally feel of gratitude for his military service, and the sterling dimensions of spirit and helpfulness he always demonstrated. All the more difficult it is to accept his untimely death.

Irresistibly comes the haunting question, "Why must my son die?"

May I share with you an exchange between a bereaved mother and a prominent author, Arthur Gordon, which *Guideposts Magazine* carried in 1968? In it, I believe, you will find spiritual help to face this loss.

Dear Mr. Gordon:

I have read your article "The Way of Acceptance" in *Guideposts,* several times, and am trying to accept the loss of a son.

Our son was killed in Vietnam on November 3, 1966, by a claymore mine while on a search and destroy mission.

He loved to help others. While stationed in Korea, he taught English in a girls' school and unofficially adopted a Korean boy whose family lived near the base, took him to the hospital several times and helped his parents, helped with clothing at an orphanage, all on his own time and money.

He told us all he wanted for Christmas that year was for us to send all the used clothing and other items we could, so he could give it to the Korean family and orphanage. How do you accept the loss of a young man who was doing and could do so much for others?

He told us about 30 percent of the men in his company were high school dropouts; he worked with them getting them to take correspondence courses so they could get their high school diplomas.

We have had letters from his friends in and out of the service, and they all spoke highly of him.

We had so much love and pride for our son. We are not young anymore and our children mean so much to us; we have only a daughter left.

Our son was coming home the last of June, and the first of July he would be coming through the door, saying, "Hi, Mom, hi, Dad!" How do we accept each day without him? An empty house, his room with all his personal possessions, a closet full of empty clothes and shoes, polished army boots and medals?

I know we are not alone in this but how do we or anyone else accept so much loss?

The weather is nice here now and he would be out swimming, playing golf or relaxing with his friends before going to his next assignment.

Our son was proud to be a soldier. I hope his life and the many thousands of others have not been sacrificed in vain.

Sincerely,
MRS. LESTER PERKINS
Oregon City, Oregon

Dear Mrs. Perkins:

I'm sure that nothing that I can say will make the anguish caused by your son's death disappear . . . only time will do this, and never fully. But perhaps I can say a few things that will help. I have never lost a child, but I lost a brother in World War II, and so I know a little bit how you feel.

It seems to me that in your grief you are making a number of very understandable mistakes.

In the first place, you are judging your son's life in terms of duration instead of quality. It was short, it's true, but it seems to me it was remarkably happy and helpful and worthwhile. These qualities are more important than any given number of days or years, aren't they?

Next, you seem to feel that your son has lost everything—the fishing and hunting that he loved, and so on. How do you know? My brother also loved to fish and hunt, as I do; in fact, that's the way I remember him most vividly . . . . Death is not simply extinction; it is moving on to something else. For all we know, your son and my brother may be hunting and fishing in better fields and streams than they ever knew here . . . or perhaps they are still helping others the way they used to do here.

Finally, I don't think your boy would want you to grieve so much. He would say, "Mom, you've got to snap out of this. We're all going to meet again, someday. In the meantime, keep my medals, but give away my clothes to somebody who can use them. Do something useful with my room; don't turn it into a shrine for grief. Some sorrow is natural, but sustained too long it becomes a destructive and self-centered thing."

Maybe acceptance is nothing more than going on bravely and cheerfully with life, no matter what happens. I'm sure that's what your son would want you to try to do.

Sincerely,

ARTHUR GORDON

Poem (*optional*)

We asked for health; now faith can see
  His radiant face; his movements swift and strong;
With every power quickened, joyously
  He plays, and has his song.

We prayed at last that he again might come
   To see the home that he held so dear,
But peacefully he reached a fairer Home
   And dearer far than here.[12]

Hymn (*optional*)   "Because He Lives" (*solo or reading by minister*)

Benediction   O God, grant us the vision of the Invisible, that in the face of death, we shall see Thee face-to-face, and rejoice in Thy presence, anticipate the reunion with loved ones and friends, and find courage and peace forevermore. In Thy holy name. *Amen.*

Postlude   "Ten Thousand Times Ten Thousand"; "O Son of Man, Our Hero"

The Lord helps them and delivers them . . . because they take refuge in him.

8

FOR ONE MISSING AND PRESUMED DEAD

Instrumental Prelude   "What a Friend We Have in Jesus"; "Great Is Thy Faithfulness"

The Opening Sentences   Trust in the LORD with all your heart, and do not rely on your own insight (Proverbs 3:5). Those who trust in the LORD are like Mount Zion, which cannot be moved but abides for ever (Psalms 125:1). The LORD helps them and delivers them . . . and saves them, because they take refuge in him (Psalms 37:40).

Invocation Prayer   Almighty God, unto whom all hearts are open, all desires known, and from whom no secrets are hid; cleanse the thoughts of our hearts by the inspiration of Thy Holy Spirit, that we may perfectly love Thee, and worthily magnify Thy holy name, through Jesus Christ our Lord. *Amen.*

Scripture Readings

From the Old Testament   When I am afraid, I put my trust in thee. In God, whose word I praise, in God I trust without a fear. What can flesh do to me? (Psalms 56:3, 4).

Whither shall I go from thy Spirit? Or whither shall I flee from thy presence? If I ascend to heaven, thou art there! If I make my bed in Sheol, thou art there! If I take the wings of the morning and dwell in the uttermost parts of the sea, even there thy hand shall lead me, and thy right hand shall hold me. If I say, "Let only darkness cover me, and the light about me be night," even the darkness is not dark to thee, the night is bright as the day; for darkness is as light with thee (Psalms 139:7–12).

O give thanks to the LORD, for he is good; his steadfast love endures for ever! . . . Out of my distress I called on the LORD; the LORD answered me and set me free. With the LORD on my side I do not fear. What can

man do to me? . . . It is better to take refuge in the
LORD than to put confidence in man. It is better to
take refuge in the LORD than to put confidence in
princes. . . . The LORD is my strength and my song;
he has become my salvation. . . . This is the LORD's
doing; it is marvelous in our eyes. This is the day which
the LORD has made; let us rejoice and be glad in it. . . .
O give thanks to the LORD, for he is good; for his steadfast love endures for ever! (Psalms 118:1–29).

He who dwells in the shelter of the Most High, who
abides in the shadow of the Almighty, will say to the
LORD, "My refuge and my fortress; my God, in whom
I trust." For he will deliver you from the snare of the
fowler and from the deadly pestilence; he will cover
you with his pinions, and under his wings you will find
refuge; his faithfulness is a shield and buckler. You will
not fear the terror of the night, nor the arrow that flies
by day, nor the pestilence that stalks in darkness, nor
the destruction that wastes at noonday. . . . Because
you have made the LORD your refuge, the Most High
your habitation, no evil shall befall you, no scourge
come near your tent. For he will give his angels charge
of you to guard you in all your ways. On their hands
they will bear you up, lest you dash your foot against
a stone (Psalms 91:1–12).

From the New Testament Faced with all this, what
can we say? If God is for us, who can be against us?
He did not even keep back his own Son, but offered
him for us all! He gave us his Son—will he not also
freely give us all things? . . . Who, then, can separate
us from the love of Christ? Can trouble do it, or hardship, or persecution, or hunger, or poverty, or danger,

or death? . . . No, in all these things we have complete victory through him who loved us! For I am certain that nothing can separate us from his love: neither death nor life; neither angels nor other heavenly rulers or powers; neither the present nor the future; neither the world above nor the world below—there is nothing in all creation that will ever be able to separate us from the love of God which is ours through Christ Jesus our Lord (Romans 8:31–39).

Poems (*optional*)

Everywhere Across the Land

Each time you look up in the sky
Or watch the fluffy clouds drift by,
Or feel the sunshine warm and bright,
Or watch the dark night turn to light,
Or hear a bluebird gaily sing
Or see the winter turn to spring,

Or stop to pick a daffodil,
Or gather violets on some hill . . .
Or touch a leaf or see a tree,
It's all GOD whispering "This is Me . . .
And I am Faith and I am Light
And in Me there shall be No Night." [13]

There's Always a Springtime

After the Winter comes the Spring
To show us again that in everything
There's always renewal divinely planned,
Flawlessly perfect, the work of God's Hand . . .
And just like the seasons that come and go
When the flowers of Spring lay buried in snow,

God sends to the heart in its winter of sadness
A springtime awakening of new hope and gladness,
And loved ones who sleep in a season of death
Will, too, be awakened by God's life-giving breath.[14]

From "The Eternal Goodness"

Yet, in the maddening maze of things,
   And tossed by storm and flood,
To one fixed trust my spirit clings;
   I know that God is good! . . .

I long for household voices gone,
   For vanished smiles I long,
But God hath led my dear ones on,
   And He can do no wrong.

I know not what the future hath
   Of marvel or surprise,
Assured alone that life and death
   His mercy underlies. . . .

And so beside the Silent Sea
   I wait the muffled oar;
No harm from Him can come to me
   On ocean or on shore.

I know not where His islands lift
   Their fronded palms in air;
I only know I cannot drift
   Beyond His love and care. . . .

And Thou, O Lord! by whom are seen
   Thy creatures as they be,
Forgive me if too close I lean
   My human heart on Thee! [15]

Pastoral Prayer   Ever-living God, the Beginner and
Sustainer of all life, the Refuge of the distressed, and

the Helper of the needy, out of the depths of our sorrow we turn to Thee.

To Thy care, All-Knowing God, we commit the life of our loved one. Help us to know, that though he is missing and is presumed dead, his whereabouts is no mystery to Thee. Help these loved ones to be assured that Thy presence shall attend him and them through the valley of doubts. Let the light of Thy countenance shine, making us feel that Thou art working even in this happening to bring about good to those who love Thee. Our light affliction is but for a moment compared to the eternal glory.

We thank Thee for the beautiful joys which have been experienced with _____, recalled in these moments. Assure us of Thy forgiveness for our neglected opportunities and thoughtless actions and words. Be merciful to us, Holy Father.

Sustain and comfort the family, until the day dawns when we shall know even as we are now fully known, when tears shall be wiped from our eyes, and death will be no more. Oh, that will be glory forever and ever, in Jesus Christ. *Amen.*

Hymn (*optional*)   "Trials Dark on Every Hand" (*solo, song by congregation, organ interlude, or reading by minister*)

Meditation   "Orchids in the Rain"

Last year our youngest daughter married. On the wedding day, from early morning to late afternoon, it rained, making it a gloomy, dismal, gray atmosphere. Especially did the wedding party, as well as the guests, find it difficult to be well groomed, wrinkle-free, and dry, for the wedding and reception were held several blocks apart. However, in no way did the storm clouds dampen the spirit and joy of the bride and groom. Even through the rain, on the way from chapel to reception, they wore their beautiful orchids. Orchids in the rain are lovely.

"When it rains, it pours" is an adage with considerable appropriateness today, for our friends are weighed down with grief and the mystery of the unknown that surrounds them. Yet there are orchids to see even in the midst of the storm. "So faith, hope, love abide, these three; but the greatest of these is love" (1 Corinthians 13:13).

Hope is like the sweet smelling orchid corsage with *faith* on the left and *love* on the right. *Hope* is the expectation of eternal good.

Hope that your loved one may still be alive somewhere.

Hope that some mistake has been made, concealing identity.

Hope that some "angel unaware" has interceded to help and sustain.

Hope in God's promises of a good future with no tears or heartache.

Hope in the eternalness of God's love. Hope is Shelley singing in the night, "If winter comes, can spring be far behind?" *Hope* is the "anchor of the soul." *Hope* is ever in the heart. When *hope* is alive, all things are alive; when *hope* is dead, all things are dead.

"So abideth *hope!*"

Faith is also an orchid that penetrates the damp darkness of the winter storm.

There is so much that we do not know about the past.

We are mystified and confused in the present. The future is hidden from our eyes. We have come to the end of human knowledge.

But *faith* would have us believe and rely upon God as the Alpha and the Omega, the beginning and the end of all things. *Faith* would assure us that we can never go anywhere and be beyond God's love and presence.

> If I take the wings of the morning and dwell in the uttermost parts of the sea, even there thy hand shall lead me, and thy right hand shall hold me.
>
> Psalms 139:9, 10

How comforting it is! *Faith* shines through the rain to lift a smile, and make beautiful the possibilities of the unknown.

John Greenleaf Whittier, that mystical poetic spirit of early American literature, catches much of our feeling today in his immortal "The Eternal Goodness." One verse reads:

> I know not where His islands lift
>   Their fronded palms in air;
> I only know I cannot drift
>   Beyond His love and care.

When you have hope and faith blooming in the rain, then there is *love* by which to live the present.

Assured of God's mercy and forgiving love, you have the spiritual help to overcome the bitterness and resentment that may linger in the dark corners of your heart. It will assuage the guilt and remorse you may harbor.

"O Love That Wilt Not Let Me Go." Such companionship of the Heavenly Father will deliver you from loneliness and self-pity, nagging enemies to the bereaved.

The Christ-love in your heart will overflow into helping others, and in that very happening a miracle of grace will take place. You will be helped and healed in the very act of helping others. We love because God first loved us.

Beatrice Decker and Gladys Koolman have written an important book entitled *After the Flowers Have Gone,* depicting the problems of the widowed. It is commendable reading for the bereaved, and the movement *Theos* which Mrs. Decker has started, is a fellowship for helping the bereaved.

One lady, whose husband died, found each morning a dreadful, distasteful—almost impossible—ordeal. It was necessary for her to work and leave her four-year-old Johnny with a sitter. She became resentful, sorry for herself. One early June morning she was awakened by a soft little hand touching her face. Then Johnny ran to the window, pulled back the curtain, and spoke with such joy, "Mommie! Mommie, look: the whole world is morning."

His voice touched a long silent chord in the mother's heart. Now, she says, when she is tempted to complain, she remembers, "This is the day the Lord has made; let us rejoice and be glad in it." Indeed, since the resurrection assurance, the whole world is morning—and the orchids are in bloom.

Benediction   To the only God, our Savior through Jesus Christ our Lord, be glory, majesty, might, and authority, from all ages past, and now, and for ever and ever! Amen (Jude 25).

Postlude   "Pass Me Not, O Gentle Savior"; "He Leadeth Me"

The years of our life are soon gone.

9

FOR ONE IN MIDDLE AGE

Instrumental Prelude   "Lord, We Come Before Thee Now"; "I Waited for the Lord" (Mendelssohn)

The Opening Sentence   The eternal God is your dwelling place, and underneath are the everlasting arms (Deuteronomy 33:27).

Invocation Prayer   Ever-living God, who can turn the sunset of death into beautiful morning, and who has set eternity in our hearts; we wait now with reverent and submissive minds, that through the harmony of music, the hope in the Scriptures, and the light of Jesus and His Resurrection, we may be brought to comfort and peace in Thy Holy Spirit. *Amen.*

Hymn (*optional*)   "Sunrise" (*solo, song by congregation, organ interlude, or reading by minister*)

Scripture Readings

From the Old Testament   Thou turnest man back to the dust, and sayest, "Turn back, O children of men!" For a thousand years in thy sight are but as yesterday when it is past, or as a watch in the night. Thou dost sweep men away; they are like a dream, like grass which is renewed in the morning: in the morning it flourishes and is renewed; in the evening it fades and withers . . . . The years of our life are threescore and ten, or even by reason of strength fourscore; yet their span is but toil and trouble; they are soon gone, and we fly away (Psalms 90:3–6; 10).

From the New Testament   I tell you the truth: the time is coming—the time has already come—when the dead will hear the voice of the Son of God, and those who hear it will live. Even as the Father is himself the source of life, in the same way he has made his Son to be the source of life. And he has given the Son the right to judge, because he is the Son of Man. Do not be surprised at this; for the time is coming when all the dead in the graves will hear his voice, and they will come out of their graves: those who have done good will be raised and live, and those who have done evil will be raised and be condemned (John 5:25–29).

Now, since our message is that Christ has been raised from death, how can some of you say that the dead will not be raised to life? If that is true, it means that Christ was not raised; and if Christ has not been raised from death, then we have nothing to preach, and you have nothing to believe. More than that, we are shown to be lying against God, because we said of him that he raised

Christ from death—but he did not raise him, if it is true that the dead are not raised to life. For if the dead are not raised, neither has Christ been raised. And if Christ has not been raised, then your faith is a delusion and you are still lost in your sins. It would also mean that the believers in Christ who have died are lost. If our hope in Christ is good for this life only, and no more, then we deserve more pity than anyone else in all the world (1 Corinthians 15:12–19).

Poems (*optional*)

Sometime, when all life's lessons have been learned,
    And suns and stars forevermore have set,
The things which our weak judgments here have spurned,
    The things o'er which we grieved with lashes wet,
Will flash before us out of life's dark night,
    As stars shine most in deeper tints of blue;
And we shall see how all God's plans were right,
    And what most seemed reproof was love most true.[16]

I know not where I'm going, but I do know my Guide,
And with childlike faith I give my hand to the Friend that's
      by my side;
The only thing I ask of him, as he takes it, is, "Hold it fast;
Suffer me not to lose my way, but bring me home at last." [17]

          There is no death;
          Our loved ones fall
          And pass away.
          They only await
          The Savior's call;
          To reign in His
          Eternal Day.[18]

Meditation   "The Assurance for Facing Death"

The keystone of the Christian faith is belief in the resurrection. Without it we come to death without meaning to life or hope beyond life. Belief in the resurrection is based upon the Resurrection of Jesus Christ, which historically has assured Christians of four great facts.

The first assurance is that *truth is stronger than falsehood*. We all recognize, whether we are Christians or not, that Jesus was a great teacher. His ideas about God and man were true. Time has vindicated them so. His enemies sought His death because they did not want their false ideas of God and goodness destroyed. If there had been no resurrection to vindicate Jesus' truth it would have meant that falsehood had obliterated truth and proved stronger than truth. The resurrection is the final assurance of the indestructibility of truth.

The second assurance that the resurrection brings is that *God is stronger than evil*. The forces that put Jesus to death were satanic. If there were no resurrection, then evil would have been triumphant. The resurrection assures that the universe is built upon moral foundations, which in the long prospective supports the good, and ultimately crumbles the wicked. With the resurrection we can be sure that goodness will prevail over evil.

The third assurance of resurrection is that *love outlasts hatred*. The greatest miscarriage of justice ever known—so shocking as to jar the moral sensibilities of the universe—was accomplished by bitter hatred. If there were no resurrection, it would mean that man's hatreds conquered the love of God. Evil men did all they could by nailing the Righteous One to a cross; but Jesus rose to live in the midst of them.

Finally, the resurrection assures us that *life is stronger than death*. If Jesus had never been raised from the dead by God's power, it would have proved that death could take the greatest life that ever lived, and break it forever. Then we might despair. The resurrection, however, convinces us that life does outlive the grave.

Jesus Himself said, "I am the resurrection and the life; he who believes in me, though he die, yet shall he live, and whoever lives and believes in me shall never die . . ." (John 11:25, 26).

Pastoral Prayer   O God eternal, the Father of the spirits of all flesh, who by a voice did proclaim, "Blessed are they who die in the Lord"; bring Thy presence to us who mourn. As we pass through the valley of the shadow, help us to gain from Thee a better understanding of life and death. Grant to the bereaved, faithful, caring friends. Lead them to the conviction of the immortality of their loved one. Grant that we may be reunited again, in that eternal home where love never loses its own, in Jesus Christ. *Amen.*

Hymn (*optional*)   "How Great Thou Art" (*solo, song by congregation, organ interlude, or reading by minister*)

Benediction   To him who is able to keep you from falling, and present you faultless and joyful before his glory—to the only God our Savior, through Jesus Christ our Lord, be glory, majesty, might, and authority, from all ages past, and now, and for ever and ever! Amen (Jude 24, 25).

Postlude   "From All That Dwell Below the Skies"

Because you are precious in my eyes.

10

FOR A YOUNG MOTHER

Instrumental Prelude "The Lord Is My Shepherd"

The Opening Sentences Let us give thanks to the God and Father of our Lord Jesus Christ, the merciful Father, the God from whom all help comes! He helps us in all our troubles, so that we are able to help those who have all kinds of troubles, using the same help that we ourselves have received from God. Just as we have a share in Christ's many sufferings, so also through Christ we share in his great help (2 Corinthians 1:3–5).

Invocation Prayer God our Father, You are able to do abundantly more than we ask or think; You have promised grace sufficient for our every need; we turn to You. You made no promise guaranteeing a fixed number of years to life; therefore, we will be thankful for what we have had. This is our time to experience a cross. We would do so bravely knowing it to be the prelude to resurrection and eternal life, assured by Jesus Christ our Lord. *Amen.*

Scripture Readings
From the Old Testament Fear not, for I am with you, be not dismayed, for I am your God; I will strengthen

you, I will help you, I will uphold you with my victorious right hand (Isaiah 41:10).

". . . Fear not, for I have redeemed you; I have called you by name, you are mine. When you pass through the waters I will be with you; and through the rivers, they shall not overwhelm you; when you walk through fire you shall not be burned, and the flame shall not consume you . . . . you are precious in my eyes, and honored, and I love you" (Isaiah 43:1–4).

From the New Testament   Jesus said to her: "I am the resurrection and the life. Whoever believes in me will live, even though he dies; and whoever lives and believes in me will never die . . ." (John 11:25, 26).

"Do not be worried and upset," Jesus told them. "Believe in God, and believe also in me. There are many rooms in my Father's house, and I am going to prepare a place for you. I would not tell you this if it were not so. And after I go and prepare a place for you, I will come back and take you to myself, so that you will be where I am. . . . If you love me, you will obey my commandments. I will ask the Father, and he will give you another Helper, the Spirit of truth, to stay with you for ever. The world cannot receive him, because it cannot see him or know him. But you know him, for he remains with you and lives in you. I will not leave you alone; I will come back to you. In a little while the world will see me no more, but you will see me; and because I live, you also will live. When that day comes, you will know that I am in my Father, and that you are in me, just as I am in you" (John 14:1–3; 15–20).

Poems (*optional*)

To Mother

You painted no Madonnas
  On chapel walls in Rome,
But with a touch diviner
  You lived them in your home.

You wrote no lofty poems
  The critics counted art,
But with a nobler vision
  You lived them in your heart.

You carved no shapeless marble
  To some high souled design,
But with a finer sculpture
  You shaped this soul of mine.

You built no great cathedrals
  That centuries applaud,
But with a grace exquisite
  Your life cathedraled God.

Had I the gift of Raphael,
  Or Michelangelo,
Oh, what a rare Madonna
  My mother's eye would show! [19]

The Soul of a Mother

Sometimes I think God grew tired of making
Thunder and mountains and dawn redly breaking;
Weary of fashioning gorges and seas,
Sometimes I think God grew tired of heating
The earth with the sun, and of fully completing
The whole of the world! God grew tired, and so
He took just a bit of the soft afterglow,

He took just a petal or two from a flower,
And took a songbird from a sweet scented bower.
The dewdrops He took from the heart of a rose,
And added the freshness of each breeze that blows
Across long green meadow. He took all the love
Left over from His heaven above.
His kind fingers mixed them—God's hand and no other—
And made, for the first time, the soul of a mother.[20]

Pastoral Prayer   O Lord, our eyes are damp with tears because of this untimely death of one we love. However, they are happy tears of gratitude for the privileged years of joy; for love of each other which is still alive this moment. You have assured us that love never eternally loses its own. We sense that we are surrounded by an invisible presence of indescribable love. So we express thankfulness.

We affirm our faith in Your promises, Heavenly Father—that every time one door closes, another door opens; that every sunset is a move closer to a new sunrise; that every evening is a time of new beginning; that death is always the prelude to resurrection; that at the end of the road is a bend leading into an exciting world of opportunity.

Comfort us then with forgiveness for our neglects and offenses. Lift us up out of the darkness, that we may stand on tiptoe and get a new view of life as You would want us. Bless the companion and children and loved ones who feel so intimately this loss, with Your love today and always, in Jesus' name. *Amen.*

Hymn (*optional*)   "Some Time We'll Understand" (*solo, song by congregation, organ interlude, or reading by minister*)

Meditation   "Gone Home"

We are met here to express appreciation for the life of a young mother, _____. She was a remarkable little homemaker, managing her household with orderly tranquility. She was a delight to know. Her eyes revealed the joy of her heart. Her laughter told us of the quality of her friendship. She made one "feel at home" in all circumstances. Her life was truly a blessing through her friendliness, her spirit of love and concern, her teaching, and above all in her dedication to God and His church. Heaven is nearer to us now since our lovely _____ is there.

Unfathomable grief cuts through our hearts, since she was snatched from us, causing rivers of tears to flow. Only the thoughts of the more blessed estate eases our grief. How much like the disciples of Jesus must be our feeling.

Friends of Jesus were deeply worried about His approaching death. What was beyond death? Would He still live? These were the questions that haunted their minds. Jesus said, in essence, "Don't worry about it. You believe in God and you have believed Me. In My Father's house are many rooms. If it were not so, would I have told you that I go to prepare a place for you?" Earth is one room; heaven is another. The door that leads from one to the other is death.

The words which comforted Jesus' friends can likewise be a comfort to us.

Thinking about the future as God's house indicates there are personal provisions prepared.

This weekend, we are having guests come to our home. My wife has been working all week to prepare a room for them. She is getting out toys their children will enjoy, the food that will meet their taste. Everything is being done with them in mind. Jesus said, "I go to prepare a place for you." The room in God's house will be personally provided, and all of God's righteous family will one day gather home.

No, not cold beneath the grasses,
    Not close-walled within the tomb;
Rather in my father's mansion,
    LIVING, in another room.

Living, like one who loves me,
    Like yon child with cheeks abloom,
Out of sight, at desk or schoolbook,
    BUSY, in another room.

Nearer than the youth whom fortune
    Beckons where the strange lands loom;
Just behind the hanging curtain,
    SERVING in another room.

Shall I doubt my Father's mercy?
    Shall I think of death as doom,
Or the stepping o'er the threshold
    To a bigger, brighter room?

Shall I blame my Father's wisdom?
    Shall I sit enswathed in gloom,
When I know my love is happy
    WAITING in another room? [21]

Seeing the future as God's house indicates also the description. It is a house of the living, full of life, where there is no death and no decay. *There shall be no more sorrow nor crying, neither shall there be any more pain.* How wonderful! No more pain! That is why death is a friend, and why this brings us consolation today.

It is a house of health and wholesomeness. It will not be a sick chamber or a hospital. There will be freedom from sin and sickness, suffering and sorrow, for the "former things are passed away." All the conditions that have afflicted the body will be over.

It will be a house of spaciousness, without the limitations of the earth.

It will be a house of reunion with friends, with the saints and with our Heavenly Father.

It will be a house that is beautiful. In Revelation 21, we read about a new heaven and a new earth, a New Jerusalem coming down from heaven as a bride adorned for her husband.

It will be an eternal house. "Though the earthly house of our tabernacle be dissolved, we have a new building of God's house, not made with hands." Here on earth there is change and decay in all that we see. Houses dissolve, empires fade, mountains crumble, but over there, God has provided for all needs.

Arthur Gossip was a man who loved his wife dearly. He was left forever in a solitude of loneliness. After this great soul contemplated her death, however, he spoke these words which have become classic: "Would you pluck the diadem from their brows again? Would you snatch the palms of victory from out of her hands? Dare you compare the clumsy nothings our poor blundering love can give her here with what she must have yonder where Christ himself has met her and heaped upon her, who can think, what happiness and glory?"

It is a prepared place for prepared people. ". . . if it were not so, would I have told you that I go to prepare a place for you?" said Jesus (John 14:2). "Whoever believes in him may have eternal life" (John 3:15).

This is not a place for everyone. It is only for those who would be at home with God, feel accepted, comfortable and loved, who are spiritually mature.

"He who believes in the Son has eternal life; he who does not obey the Son shall not see life . . ." (John 3:36).

Are you prepared for this prepared place? If we can trust Jesus at all, and certainly we can, then, today comfort your hearts by knowing that _____ has gone to her heavenly home.

Hymn (*optional*) "One Sweetly Solemn Thought" (*solo, song by congregation, organ interlude, or reading by minister*)

Benediction Paul said: ". . . the one thing I do, however, is to forget what is behind me and do my best to reach what is ahead. So I run straight toward the goal in order to win the prize, which is God's call through Christ Jesus to the life above. All of us who are spiritually mature should have this same attitude . . ." (Philippians 3:13–15).

O God—may it be so. *Amen.*

Postlude "Servant of God, Well Done"; "Forever With the Lord"

Do not be afraid of those who kill the body but cannot kill the soul.

11

FOR AN ACCIDENT VICTIM

Instrumental Prelude   "Consolation" (Mendelssohn); "O Sacred Head Now Wounded"

The Opening Sentences   Cast your burden on the LORD, and he will sustain you . . . (Psalms 55:22).

Our help is in the name of the LORD, who made heaven and earth (Psalms 124:8).

To thee, O LORD, I lift up my soul. O my God, in thee I trust . . . (Psalms 25:1, 2).

Invocation Prayer   O God, by whose wisdom life has come, by whose power the provisions for existence have been supplied, by whose mysterious presence communication is possible, in whose grace is our future, we bow in gratitude for Jesus Christ who brought life and immortality to light—and taught us the concerns of prayer, praying:

Unison Lord's Prayer   Our Father, who art in heaven, hallowed be Thy Name. Thy kingdom come, Thy will be done on earth as it is in heaven. Give us this day our daily bread; And forgive us our debts, as we forgive our debtors. And lead us not into temptation, but deliver us from evil; For Thine is the kingdom, and the power, and the glory, forever. *Amen.*

Scripture Readings

From the Old Testament   When my soul was embittered, when I was pricked in heart, I was stupid and ignorant, I was like a beast toward thee. Nevertheless I am continually with thee; thou dost hold my right hand. Thou dost guide me with thy counsel, and afterward thou wilt receive me to glory. Whom have I in heaven but thee? And there is nothing upon earth that I desire besides thee. My flesh and my heart may fail, but God is the strength of my heart and my portion for ever (Psalms 73:21–26).

Remember also your Creator in the days of your youth, before the evil days come, and the years draw nigh, when you will say, "I have no pleasure in them"; before the sun and the light and the moon and the stars are darkened and the clouds return after the rain; in the day when the keepers of the house tremble, and the strong men are bent, and the grinders cease because they are few, and those that look through the windows are dimmed, and the doors on the street are shut; when the sound of the grinding is low, and one rises up at the voice of a bird . . . . before the silver cord is snapped, or the golden bowl is broken, or the pitcher is broken at the fountain, or the wheel broken at the cistern, and the dust returns to the earth as it was, and the spirit returns to God who gave it (Ecclesiastes 12:1–7).

From the New Testament   There is no need to write you, brothers, about the times and occasions when these things will happen. For you yourselves know very well that the Day of the Lord will come like a thief comes at night. When people say, "Everything is quiet and safe," then suddenly destruction will hit them! They will not escape—it will be like the pains that come upon a woman who is about to give birth. But you, brothers, are not in the darkness, and the Day should not take you by surprise like a thief. All of you are people who belong to the light, who belong to the day. . . . We must wear faith and love as a breast-plate, and our hope of salvation as a helmet. God did not choose us to suffer his wrath, but to possess salvation through our Lord Jesus Christ, who died for us in order that we might live together with him, whether are alive or dead when he comes. For this reason encourage one another, and help one another, just as you are now doing (1 Thessalonians 5:1–11).

"Do not be afraid of those who kill the body but cannot kill the soul; rather be afraid of God, who can destroy both body and soul in hell. You can buy two sparrows for a penny; yet not a single one of them falls to the ground without your Father's consent. As for you, even the hairs of your head have all been counted. So do not be afraid: you are worth much more than sparrows!" (Matthew 10:28–31).

For just as all men die because of their union to Adam, in the same way all will be raised to life because of their union to Christ. But each one in his proper order: Christ, the first of all; then those who belong to Christ, at the time of his coming. Then the end will come; Christ will overcome all spiritual rulers, authorities, and powers, and hand over the Kingdom to God the Father. For Christ must rule until God defeats all enemies and puts them under his feet. The last enemy to be defeated will be death (1 Corinthians 15:22–26).

Faced with all this, what can we say? If God is for us, who can be against us? He did not even keep back his own Son, but offered him for us all! He gave us his Son—will he not also freely give us all things? Who will accuse God's chosen people? God himself declares them not guilty! Can anyone, then, condemn them? Christ Jesus is the one who died, or rather, who was raised to life and is at the right side of God. He pleads with God for us! Who, then, can separate us from the love of Christ? Can trouble do it, or hardship, or persecution, or hunger, or poverty, or danger, or death? . . . No, in all these things we have complete victory through him who loved us! For I am certain that nothing can separate us from his love: neither death nor life; neither angels nor other heavenly rulers or powers; neither the present nor the future; neither the world above nor the world below—there is nothing in all creation that will ever be able to separate us from the love of God which is ours through Christ Jesus our Lord (Romans 8:31–39).

Poems (*optional*)

Something has spoken in the night . . .
And told me I shall die, I know not where.
Saying:

"To lose the earth you know, for greater knowing:
To lose the life you have, for greater life;

To leave the friends you loved, for greater loving:
To find a land more kind than home, more large
than earth—" [22]

I will not doubt, though all my ships at sea
  Come drifting home with broken masts and sails;
  I shall believe the Hand which never fails,
For seeming evil worketh good for me;
  And, though I weep because these sails are battered,
  Still will I cry, while my best hopes lie shattered,
"I trust in Thee!" [23]

Not now, but in the coming years
  It may be in the better land,
We'll read the meaning of our tears
  And there, some time, we'll understand.[24]

Pastoral Prayer Heavenly Father, who has assured us that not even a sparrow falls to the ground without Your knowledge, comfort these here gathered with the knowledge of Your concern and nearness.

We thank You for the life of _____, for his abilities; for his well-directed influences; for the discipline and clearness of his manner; for his love of family; for his work with youth; for his participation in the church.

Inscribe these golden memories on the canvas of our minds that we might be renewed from the inspiration of his life.

O Thou of tender mercy, who art able to do more than we think about or pray for, sustain these friends through this grief experience, that this loss may be assimilated into life. Grant to the sons and to the daughters a double portion of their father's good qualities.

O Spirit of Christ, save us all, and the family espe-

cially, we pray, from the cancer of bitterness and resentment that envelops the heart; from hostility and
anger that clouds the soul, from guilt that is self-
destructive, from the grief that paralyzes hope.

Bind up our inward wounds eternally by faith, hope,
and love demonstrated in the cross where Thine own
dear Son died, young and undeservingly, for us. *Amen.*

Hymn (*optional*)   "It Is Well With My Soul" (*solo,
song by congregation, organ interlude, or reading by
minister*)

Meditation   "Fearing the Right Enemies"

Stunned with shock from such an unwelcomed intru-
sion as death, numbed with sadness because the beautiful life of _____ has been cut down by accident in
the midst of his most productive years, we meet here
to honor his memory. We express gratitude for our
cherished associations with him, and will attempt to
put this loss in a perspective that will ease the pain and
kindle hope in our hearts.

"Why did this happen?" you ask. "Why did not God
do something to stop it?" We can never completely
understand life's tragedies. This we do know—God has
given man the freedom of human choice from which
comes his noblest attainments as well as his cruelest
tragedies. From it comes man's development as conscious, moral individuals, but also from man's disobedience and poor judgment come damaging accidents.
Such is this case. Human frailty and misuse of freedom
has brought hurt and death to many innocent victims.
Surely it was God's intention that _____ live out a
full, complete life. Not God, but man is to be held

responsible for this sudden termination. The evil of one spills over into the lives of others. So, for the sake of others we are called to maturity, to self-control and obedience in the use of freedom, according to the Spirit of Jesus Christ.

Gratefully, we affirm the reality of eternal life. ". . . because I live," said Jesus, "you will live also" (John 14:19). For God has turned our sunsets into sunrise, our bad news into good news, our despair into hope. Our earthly journey, however long or short, is but a few years in the timetable of God's eternity. For but a little while we are in this nursery and elementary school of heaven. Here life receives its direction. If we have committed our dreams and desires, our concerns and character toward the authentic ideal in Jesus Christ, then we shall have life beyond this earthly span. If we are developing spiritual capacities that are at-one with God's love, at home in his home, then we shall find our place in the place he has prepared for those who love and obey Him and are perfected in Him.

If we have not developed these Christlike capacities and calloused wickedness rules our lives, if we have neglected the soul and assume the body is ultimate, then we perish with that which is perishable. This is the second death—that is, spiritual death. "God so loved the world that he gave his only Son, that whoever believes in him should not perish . . ." (John 3:16).

Little wonder that Jesus admonishes, "Do not fear those who kill the body . . ." (Matthew 10:28)— rather fear the influences and temptations that destroy both the soul and the body, for the wicked shall perish.

These bodies are mere houses for our spirits—physi-

cal mediums for the transmission of our personalities—
the organs by which we communicate and relate to one
another. When the physical body is destroyed by accident, or hampered by disease, or outworn by age, do
not despair. It is not final disaster, for as Jesus said,
". . . he who believes in me, though he die, yet shall
he live, and whoever lives and believes in me shall
never [spiritually] die" (John 11:25, 26).

John Quincy Adams, when old in years, was once
asked how he was. "John Quincy Adams is very well,
sir, very well. The house in which he has been living so
many years is dilapidated and old. He has received
word from the owner that he must vacate soon—but
John Quincy Adams is very well, sir, very well."

Benediction   To him who is able to keep you from
falling, and present you faultless and joyful before his
glory—to the only God our Savior, through Jesus Christ
our Lord, be glory, majesty, might, and authority, from
all ages past, and now, and for ever and ever! Amen
(Jude 24, 25).

Postlude   "God Be With You"

If we share Christ's suffering, we will also share his glory.

12

FOR A CANCER VICTIM

Instrumental Prelude   "Sun of My Soul, Thou Savior Dear"; "Day Is Dying in the West"

The Opening Sentences   For everything there is a season, and a time for every matter under heaven: a time to be born, and a time to die; a time to plant, and a time to pluck up what is planted . . . a time to weep, and a time to laugh; a time to mourn, and a time to dance (Ecclesiastes 3:1–4). What no man ever saw or heard, What no man ever thought could happen, Is the very thing God prepared for those who love him (1 Corinthians 2:9).

Invocation Prayer   God eternal, immortal, and invisible, who cannot be seen with the eyes of flesh, grant that we may behold Thee with the eyes of faith. We thank Thee that death to our friend has meant release from the trials and pain and fear of this mortal life and is an entrance into that unspeakable joy which Thou hast promised to those who love Thy Son, our Lord Jesus Christ, in whose name we pray. *Amen.*

Scripture Readings

From the Old Testament   The LORD is my shepherd, I shall not want; he makes me lie down in green pastures. He leads me beside still waters; he restores my soul. He leads me in paths of righteousness for his name's sake.

Even though I walk through the valley of the shadow of death, I fear no evil; for thou art with me; thy rod and thy staff, they comfort me.

Thou preparest a table before me in the presence of my enemies; thou anointest my head with oil, my cup overflows. Surely goodness and mercy shall follow me all the days of my life; and I shall dwell in the house of the LORD for ever (Psalm 23).

From the New Testament   So then, my brothers, we have an obligation, but not to live as our human nature wants us to. For if you live according to your human nature, you are going to die; but if, by the Spirit, you kill your sinful actions, you will live. Those who are led by God's Spirit are God's sons. For the Spirit that God has given you does not make you a slave and cause you to be afraid; instead, the Spirit makes you God's sons, and by the Spirit's power we cry to God, "Father! my Father!" God's Spirit joins himself to our spirits to declare that we are God's children. Since we are his children, we will possess the blessings he keeps for his people, and we will also possess with Christ what God has kept for him; for if we share Christ's suffering, we will also share his glory.

I consider that what we suffer at this present time cannot be compared at all with the glory that is going to be revealed to us. All of creation waits with eager longing for God to reveal his sons. For creation was condemned to become worthless, not of its own will, but because God willed it to be so. Yet there was this hope: that creation itself would one day be set free from its slavery to decay, and share the glorious freedom of the children of God. For we know that up to the present time all of creation groans with pain like the pain of childbirth. But not just creation alone; we who have the Spirit as the first of God's gifts, we also groan within ourselves as we wait for God to make us his sons and set our whole being free. For it was by hope that we were saved; but if we see what we hope for, then it is not really hope. For who hopes for something that he sees? But if we hope for what we do not see, we wait for it with patience (Romans 8:12–25).

And this small and temporary trouble we suffer will bring us a tremendous and eternal glory, much greater than the trouble. For we fix our attention, not on things that are seen, but on things that are unseen. What can be seen lasts only for a time; but what cannot be seen lasts for ever (2 Corinthians 4:17, 18).

Then I saw a new heaven and a new earth. The first heaven and the first earth disappeared, and the sea vanished. And I saw the Holy City, the new Jerusalem, coming down out of heaven from God, prepared and ready, like a bride dressed to meet her husband. I heard a loud voice speaking from the throne: "Now God's home is with men! He will live with them, and they shall be his people. God himself will be with them, and he will be their God. He will wipe away all tears from their eyes. There will be no more death, no more grief, crying, or pain. The old things have disappeared" (Revelation 21:1–4).

Poems (*optional*)

No More Death

No more death; no more sorrow, and no fears;
   No valley of the shadow, no more pain!
No weeping, for God dries away the tears,
   And dried by him tears never rise again.

No darkened room, no silence, and no cry
   Of bitterness as he recalls the breath;
No unfilled blank, no nameless agony;
   For he hath said, "There shall be no more death."

No more death! Then take comfort, ye who weep
   Give thanks to God, and raise the bowed head;
They are not lost—'tis his beloved sleep,
   And he who takes and keeps the holy dead.

Are they not safe with him? And when the veil
   Is rent for us, and sight supplanteth faith,
Then, reunited, love shall never fail;
   For he hath said, "There shall be no more death." [25]

Pastoral Prayer Most merciful God, who art from everlasting to everlasting; in these quiet moments speak to us of eternal things. Our spirits sink before the mystery of suffering and death. Look with compassion upon this sorrowing family who have been so attentive and faithful in the care of their loved one. Remembering all Thy mercies, Thy promises, and Thy love in Christ, may their sorrow be lessened, and their hope brightened. Thou hast promised eternal life in the Gospel of Thy Son, Jesus Christ, and confirmed it to us by His Resurrection. Thou hast promised a world where there is no more pain, and where parting is unknown. Thank You Lord for this assurance. Cheered by these hopes, we would commit our beloved dead into Thy holy and merciful keeping, believing that, though we see them no more, they are safe with Thee, and rest from their labors, relieved of anguish and at peace.

Reunite us forevermore, we pray, in the house of many rooms. *Amen.*

Hymn (*optional*)   "Now the Day Is Over" (*solo, song by congregation, organ interlude, or reading by minister*)

Meditation   "The Great Commencement"

Our brother (sister) died at the age of _____. It would be more appropriate to say, he began to live the eternal life at _____, for from the Christian perspective death is a commencement.

Though we are never completely ready for the separation that death brings and we sorrow in parting, yet from a larger view it is a merciful release. Our friend has endured long the suffering of his illness which could only have increased with the passing days. He has faced frustration, confinement, sleepless nights, discouragement, limitation of expression, helplessness. Death has terminated this unhappy estate. It has brought his spirit release from this earthly environment. He is now free to begin life in new dimensions.

If we have faith in the Christian promise, can we not be reconciled by the awareness that the earthly life is not the total book of personal existence, only the opening chapter? not our total existence, only preparation for the whole life? not the house, only the porch of the Father's mansion!

As the fertile growth of spring, the sunlit days of summer and the light frost of autumn prepare the leaves for their winter departure, so through the seasons of our lives God prepares us at the appropriate time to leave this world, so we may enter the "world without end."

One lady who had been ill for many months said to her pastor, "I am ready to start the journey. The possibilities of what lie ahead excite me." That is great faith with which to face death.

If we would face death in such a manner, there are two things necessary to develop. First, a profound assurance that this life on earth is not the full measure and limit to what God intends our dwelling place to be.

The other factor is to know how to find the way to the better world. Jesus said to the skeptical Thomas, "I am the way, and the truth, and the life . . ." (John 14:6). When one discovers these factors, he is then ready for death. Old Simeon said in the Temple when at last he saw the Christ-child, "Lord, now lettest thou thy servant depart in peace, according to thy word; for mine eyes have seen thy salvation" (Luke 2:29, 30). Saint Paul found the secret to life, then he declared, "My desire is to depart and be with Christ, for that is far better" (Philippians 1:23). "For to me to live is Christ, and to die is gain" (Philippians 1:21).

For all who have discovered these two things, death is not really death at all; it is a marvelous release to life. "Whoever lives and believes in me shall never die" (John 11:26).

Victor Hugo said it this way, "For half a century I have been writing my thoughts in prose and in verse; history, philosophy, drama, romance, tradition, satire, ode and song; I have tried all. But I feel I have not said the thousandth part of what is in me. When I go down to the grave I can say, like many others, 'I have finished my day's work.' But I can not say, 'I have finished my life.' My day's work will begin again the next morning. The tomb is not a blind alley; it is a thoroughfare. It closes in the twilight, and opens in the dawn."

Benediction May our passing days be rich in those things which death cannot take away from us; and do Thou, O Lord, strengthen us to live a life of faith and righteousness, of love and service which will make this earthly change but a step nearer to Thee and our eternal home, through Jesus Christ our Lord. *Amen.*

Postlude "Sunset and Evening Star"; "Come, Sweet Repose" (Bach)

God is our refuge and strength, a very present help in time of trouble.

13

FOR A MURDER VICTIM

Instrumental Prelude "There's a Wideness in God's Mercy"; "Nearer my God to Thee"; "Safe in the Arms of Jesus"

The Opening Sentence   Our help is in the name of the
LORD, who made heaven and earth (Psalms 124:8).

Invocation Prayer   Almighty God, our Heavenly
Father, unto whom all hearts are open, all desires
known, from whom no secrets are hidden, and whose
judgments are inscrutable; in our deep distress we turn
to Thee. Thou art able to do abundantly more than we
ask or think, so we place ourselves and our circumstances into Thy hands, trusting Thy all-encompassing
knowledge, Thy never-changing righteousness, Thy
measureless love, and Thy proven power to right all
wrongs, and to vindicate at last, all justice, through
Jesus Christ our Lord, who though unjustly killed, lives
eternally. *Amen.*

Scripture Readings
From the Old Testament   "LORD, let me know my end,
and what is the measure of my days; let me know how
fleeting my life is! . . . And now, Lord, for what do I
wait? My hope is in thee. Deliver me from all my transgressions. Make me not the scorn of the fool! . . .
Hear my prayer, O LORD, and give ear to my cry; hold
not thy peace at my tears! For I am thy passing guest,
a sojourner, like all my fathers" (Psalms 39:4–12).

God is our refuge and strength, a very present help
in trouble. Therefore we will not fear though the earth
should change, though the mountains shake in the heart
of the sea; though its waters roar and foam, though the
mountains tremble with its tumult. . . . "Be still, and
know that I am God. I am exalted among the nations,
I am exalted in the earth!" The LORD of hosts is with
us; the God of Jacob is our refuge (Psalms 46:1–11).

From the New Testament At that time Jesus said: "O Father, Lord of heaven and earth! I thank you because you have shown to the unlearned what you have hidden from the wise and learned. Yes, Father, this was done by your own choice and pleasure.

"My Father has given me all things. No one knows the Son except the Father, and no one knows the Father except the Son, and those to whom the Son wants to reveal him.

"Come to me, all of you who are tired from carrying your heavy loads, and I will give you rest. Take my yoke and put it on you, and learn from me, for I am gentle and humble in spirit; and you will find rest. The yoke I will give you is easy, and the load I will put on you is light" (Matthew 11:25–30).

Have your minds ready for action, then. Keep alert, and set your hope completely on the blessing which will be given you when Jesus Christ is revealed. Be obedient to God, and do not allow your lives to be shaped by those desires that you had when you were still ignorant. Instead, be holy in all that you do, just as God who called you is holy. For the scripture says, "You must be holy, because I am holy."

You call him Father, when you pray to God, who judges all men alike, according to what each one has done; you must, therefore, spend the rest of your lives here on earth in reverence for him. For you know what was paid to set you free from the worthless manner of life you received from your ancestors. It was not something that loses its value, such as silver or gold; you were set free by the costly sacrifice of Christ, who was like a lamb without defect or spot. He had been chosen by God before the creation of the world, and was re-vealed in these last days for your sake. Through him you believe in God, who raised him from death and gave him glory; and so your faith and hope are fixed on God (1 Peter 1:13–21).

Hymn (*optional*)   "I Need Thee Every Hour" (*solo, song by congregation, organ interlude, or reading by minister*)

Pastoral Prayer   O Thou, Eternal One, who has said, "Vengeance is mine; I will repay," in this great afflic-tion we turn to Thee. Our Father, comfort these stricken people upon whom this tragedy has come. Sustain them in the Spirit of Jesus, that they may be delivered from bitterness, hatred, and vengeance. Mellow their spirits with the Spirit of Jesus who forgave even those who murdered Him. We trust Thee, O God, to enlighten our darkness, and to bring us out of our distress.

Grant, O Lord, that from henceforth we may give ourselves to Thee, and having given ourselves, may give our abilities to teach Thy ways to others, until Thy kingdom of love, reverence, and goodwill may spread through human hearts everywhere upon the earth.

Now we commend the soul of our departed to Thy loving care. *Amen.*

Meditation   "Someday We Will Understand"
My dear friends, let not your hearts be troubled with questions whose full answers can never be found here upon earth. "For now we see in a mirror dimly, but then face to face. Now I know in part; then I shall understand fully, even as I have been fully understood" (1 Corinthians 13:12).

When death strikes suddenly, by some tragic, bewildering process, our minds question *why*. A multitude of questions involving the motive and ways of God, and the future estate of our loved ones surface in our thought. The death of _____ has raised many difficult problems for this family to resolve. It is a fruitless inquiry, for as the Apostle Paul said, "Now we see in a mirror dimly. . . ." We can never prove, in a scientific laboratory, the nature of God, or the soul, or the substance of the spiritual. Many of life's most profound realities we assimilate into life before achieving scientific proof. Clearly we do not know the whole story. However, the promise is that one day we shall know and understand, even as God now understands us.

We have glimpses of truth in Jesus Christ, ". . . who abolished death and brought life and immortality to light" (2 Timothy 1:10).

Our religious faith teaches us that we live our present life in a world that is not our true home. We live in a sin-infested, evil-ruined, sorrow-filled world. The rebellious, disobedient nature of man has destroyed the Garden of Eden and the intention of God.

But God loves us with an everlasting love. "God so loved the world that he gave his only Son, that whoever believes in him should not perish but have eternal life" (John 3:16).

Benediction   And God's peace, which is far beyond human understanding, will keep your hearts and minds safe, in Christ Jesus (Philippians 4:7). *Amen.*

Postlude   "Jesus, Saviour Pilot Me"; "Guide Me, O Thou Great Jehovah"

Fear not, for I am with you.

14

FOR A SUICIDE VICTIM

Instrumental Prelude "Rock of Ages"; "Come to Me" (Beethoven)

The Opening Sentences Comfort, comfort my people, says your God . . . . "You are my servant, I have chosen you and not cast you off"; fear not, for I am with you, be not dismayed, for I am your God; I will strengthen you, I will help you, I will uphold you with my victorious right hand . . . . For I, the LORD your God, hold your right hand; it is I who say to you, "Fear not, I will help you" (Isaiah 40:1; 41:9–13).

Invocation Prayer Almighty God, our heavenly Father, who art the dwelling place and home of thy people in all generations, have mercy upon us as we draw near to thee under the shadow of great affliction, for in thee alone is our confidence and hope . . . Look in tender pity on thy bereaved servants, and enable them by thy grace to find in thee their refuge and their strength . . . in the name of him, who is the resurrection and the life, even Jesus Christ our Lord. *Amen.*[26]

Scripture Readings

From the Old Testament O LORD, thou hast searched me and known me! Thou knowest when I sit down and when I rise up; thou discernest my thoughts from afar. Thou searchest out my path and my lying down, and art acquainted with all my ways . . . . Whither shall I go from thy Spirit? Or whither shall I flee from thy presence? If I ascend to heaven, thou art there! If I make my bed in Sheol, thou art there! If I take the wings of the morning and dwell in the uttermost parts of the sea, even there thy hand shall lead me, and thy right hand shall hold me. If I say, "Let only darkness cover me, and the light about me be night, even the darkness is not dark to thee, the night is bright as the day; for darkness is as light with thee . . . . Search me, O God, and know my heart! Try me and know my thoughts! And see if there be any wicked way in me, and lead me in the way everlasting! (Psalms 139:1–24).

From the New Testament But do not forget this one thing, my dear friends! There is no difference in the Lord's sight between one day and a thousand years; to him the two are the same. The Lord is not slow to do what he has promised, as some think. Instead, he is patient with you, because he does not want anyone to be destroyed, but wants all to turn away from their sins.

But the Day of the Lord will come as a thief. On that Day the heavens will disappear with a shrill noise, the heavenly bodies will burn up and be destroyed, and the earth with everything in it will vanish . . . . And so, my friends, as you wait for that Day, do your best to be pure and faultless in God's sight and to be at peace with him (2 Peter 3:8–14).

Pastoral Prayer   Father of mercies and God of all comfort, the author of life on both sides of death; we cast all our cares upon Thee, for Thou dost care for us.

We remember the frailty and uncertainty of our life. Thou alone dost understand the depths of human despair. Thou art ever compassionate toward the depressed and the sick in body and mind. From Thee no secrets are hidden. In Thy love and wisdom, forgive the wrongs and injustices.

We commit to Thy fatherly care him who has been crushed by the chaos of the world and tortured in mind and spirit by its pressure and confusion.

Merciful Father, by Thy Spirit, comfort these upon whom this trial and loss has come. Be their strength and shield, a very present help in this time of trouble, so they may be delivered at last from bitterness, guilt, despair. Be to them the light to brighten their darkness of loneliness and doubt.

Grant us the sensitivity and compassion that we may help those in need of cheer, comfort and friendship, thus to be servants of Jesus Christ, our Lord. *Amen.*

Hymn (*optional*)   "When I Survey the Wondrous Cross" (*solo, song by congregation, organ interlude, or reading by minister*)

Meditation   "Think About These Things"

This man was my friend. He was your friend. He was loved by his family. So let us remember all the good that we can recall.

It is not our prerogative to dictate ecclesiastical judgments, nor to intimate destiny. This is within the realm of the all-knowing, just, and loving God who knows all circumstances, from beginning to end. Upon His grace we are cast.

As a household of faith, we come to convey Christian love to the family, to share your loss, and to pray for God's guidance and support.

Wise would we be to heed the Apostle Paul's admonition when he wrote in Philippians 4:8 to "think about these things": whatever is true, whatever is honorable, whatever is just, whatever is pure, whatever is lovely, whatever is gracious. If there is any excellence, anything worthy of praise, think about these things.

There is something fine in every person which is worthy of appreciation, and should be etched deeply upon the canvas of the mind.

Burdened with this new sorrow, feverish and sick at heart, you perhaps ask, "Where shall I find help? Who can comfort me?"

In the Master's supreme agony, as the shadow of the cross became clear and His betrayal was at hand, when He prayed for escape and sweat great drops of blood, Luke's Gospel records, "There appeared to him an angel from heaven, strengthening him" (Luke 22:43).

God still ministers to His people. It may be through friends and relatives who have empathy and sincere love who enter into your sorrow, thus easing the burden. Or it may be through "angels unaware," through spiritual resources and heavenly assistance that causes the heart to sing even in darkest nights. Jesus' promise to His beloved is, "I will not leave you desolate . . . I will pray the Father, and he will give another Coun-

selor, to be with you for ever, even the Spirit of truth
. . . you know him, for he dwells with you, and will
be in you . . . The Counselor, the Holy Spirit, whom
the Father will send in my name . . . . Peace I leave
with you; my peace I give to you . . . . Let not your
hearts be troubled, neither let them be afraid" (John
14:16–27).

Benediction May God the Father and Christ Jesus
our Lord give you grace, mercy, and peace (1 Timothy
1:2).

Postlude "Abide With Me"

*The Lord has anointed me to bring good
tidings to the afflicted.*

15

FOR ONE WHO HAD
MENTAL ILLNESS

Instrumental Prelude "In the Hour of Trial"; "What
a Friend We Have in Jesus"

The Opening Sentences "Come to me, all of you who
are tired from carrying your heavy loads, and I will give
you rest. Take my yoke and put it on you, and learn
from me, for I am gentle and humble in spirit; and you

will find rest. The yoke I will give you is easy, and the load I will put on you is light" (Matthew 11:28–30).

Invocation Prayer   O God, our Heavenly Father, to whom we may come in every hour of darkness and sorrow, we pour out our griefs and rest our troubled hearts under the shelter of Thy compassion. We thank Thee for Jesus Christ. We pray for the assurance of His life, that the sorrows of death are but for a little while, and the grave is only a gate of entrance to another world where joy, peace, and love abide. Guide the words of our mouths and the meditation of our hearts, O Lord, our strength and Redeemer. *Amen.*

Scripture Readings

From the Old Testament   The Spirit of the Lord GOD is upon me, because the LORD has anointed me to bring good tidings to the afflicted; he has sent me to bind up the brokenhearted, to proclaim liberty to the captives, and the opening of the prison to those who are bound; to proclaim the year of the LORD's favor, and the day of vengeance of our God; to comfort all who mourn; to grant to those who mourn in Zion—to give them a garland instead of ashes, the oil of gladness instead of mourning, the mantle of praise instead of a faint spirit; that they may be called oaks of righteousness, the planting of the LORD, that he may be glorified (Isaiah 61: 1–3).

From the New Testament   For this reason we never become discouraged. Even though our physical being is gradually decaying, yet our spiritual being is renewed day after day. And this small and temporary trouble we suffer will bring us a tremendous and eternal glory, much greater than the trouble. For we fix our attention, not on things that are seen, but on things that are unseen. What can be seen lasts only for a time; but what cannot be seen lasts for ever.

For we know that when this tent we live in—our body here on earth—is torn down, God will have a house in heaven for us to live in, a home he himself made, which will last for ever. And now we sigh, so great is our desire to have our home which is in heaven put on over us; for by being clothed with it we shall not be found without a body. While we live in this earthly tent we groan with a feeling of oppression; it is not that we want to get rid of our earthly body, but that we want to have the heavenly one put on over us, so that what is mortal will be swallowed up by life. God is the one who has prepared us for this change, and he gave us his Spirit as the guarantee of all that he has for us.

So we are always full of courage. We know that as long as we are at home in this body we are away from the Lord's home. For our life is a matter of faith, not of sight. We are full of courage, and would much prefer to leave our home in this body and be at home with the Lord. More than anything else, however, we want to please him, whether in our home here or there. For all of us must appear before Christ, to be judged by him, so that each one may receive what he deserves, according to what he has done, good or bad, in his bodily life (2 Corinthians 4:16; 5:1–10).

. . . He who sits on the throne will protect them with his presence. Never again will they hunger or thirst; neither sun nor any scorching heat will burn

them; for the Lamb, who is in the center of the throne
will be their shepherd, and guide them to springs of
living water; and God will wipe away every tear from
their eyes" (Revelation 7:15–17).

Poems (*optional*)

> O say, "He has arrived!"
> And not that "He has gone."
> May every thought of him
> Be in that Land of Morn.
>
> Arrived! To hear His voice
> And see His welcoming smile;
> And then to greet again
> Those he has lost a while.
>
> Arrived! To tread no more
> The weary path of pain,
> Nor feel the waning strength
> The body feels, again.
>
> To be forever free
> From all that limits love,
> In joyful service thus
> He now may tireless move.
>
> Then say not, "He has gone,"
> Nor think of him as dead;
> But say, "In the Father's House
> He has arrived!"—instead.[27]

Pastoral Prayer   O God, our Lord, the comforter of
those who put their trust in Thee, be Thou our friend.
Even when we walk through the dark valley, Thy light
can shine into our hearts and guide us through the
night of shadow.

May we who remain behind ever keep clear and bright the beautiful memory of the one who has gone to be with Thee. We are grateful for the merciful release which death has brought from fear, confusion, and anguish. We would accept the sorrow without murmuring, because of the consolation and joy from hope in Thee.

Lord, give peace to the troubled, forgiveness to the remorseful, strength to the weak, love to the lonely. Lead all of us by the still waters of comfort and in the paths of righteousness, until we rest in Thy kingdom of glory, in Jesus' name. *Amen.*

Hymn (*optional*) "Face-to-Face" (*solo, song by congregation, organ interlude, or reading by minister*)

Meditation "Healing for the Broken Heart"

When Jesus was asked to read the Scripture lesson in his home synagogue in Nazareth, He turned to the passage in Isaiah 61 which described His ministry. One of the reasons He had come was to "heal the brokenhearted." He was an ambassador of God's comforts.

Our Lord understood people. He realized the burdens they carried. Once He said, "Come to me, all who labor and are heavy laden, and I will give you rest" (Matthew 11:28).

He bids us come to Him, for herein is our comfort.

One of the ways in which He "heals the brokenhearted" (Psalms 147:3) is helping us keep sorrow and suffering in proper perspective. No matter how overmastering some of our experiences may seem, they need not defeat us.

In 2 Corinthians 4:17, Paul puts it this way: "For

this slight momentary affliction is preparing for us an eternal weight of glory beyond all comparison, because we look not to the things that are seen but to the things that are unseen; for the things that are seen are transient, but the things that are unseen are eternal."

Look at the contrasts in that sentence: "slight momentary affliction" and "an eternal weight of glory." Though the pain and discomfort of affliction seems a terrible ordeal, yet God uses it to help us grow and deepen spiritually and attain "an eternal weight of glory."

Look at the words *momentary* and *eternal*. Though the suffering has seemed long, it was for just a moment in contrast to the world without end.

Or again, see the contrast in *seen* and *unseen, transient* and *eternal*. That which we see is not the true reality. The world of the unseen is more real than we have ever known.

If we can keep perspective, we shall be comforted.

Jesus heals the brokenhearted, by bidding us to recall the blessed days of fellowship and companionship. Do not try to forget those who leave us. Do not put the days of joy and happiness out of your conversation and thoughts. Indeed, we have come here to recall the good gift God has given us in sharing the life and character of _____. (*Review some of the enduring characteristics of the departed.*)

Jesus heals the brokenhearted by reminding us of the wonderful deliverance that death brings.

In Revelation 21:4 we read, "he [God] will wipe away every tear from their eyes, and death shall be no more, neither shall there be mourning nor crying nor pain any more, for the former things have passed away."

Tears are a symbol of suffering. Earth is mingled with smiles and tears, joy and sorrow.

God wipes away all tears. There is no more exposure to hunger, thirst, sickness, death, or tears. All bodily conditions and limitations are overcome.

His love prompts it. His purpose determines it. His power secures it. Praise be to God!

Some years ago, a dear friend of mine endured the death of his wife. She had a long lingering bout with illness. When finally she was taken, he said to me, "God has healed her, by taking her." It confused me at the moment, yet in retrospect it is true. Death was relief from the burden of a diseased body and distraught mind. God brought eternal healing for her spirit. He set her free for continued growth. So with your dear one.

Hymn (*optional*)   "Beyond the Sunset" (*solo, song by congregation, organ interlude, or reading by minister*)

Benediction

> O Thou who hearest prayer,
> Give ear unto our cry;
> O let Thy children share
> Thy blessings from on high.
> We plead the promise of Thy word,
> O grant us peace, Almighty Lord.[28]

May grace and peace be yours in full measure, through your knowledge of God and of Jesus our Lord (2 Peter 1:2). *Amen.*

Postlude   "Eye Hath Not Seen"; "God Shall Wipe Away All Tears"

If Thou, O Lord, shouldst mark iniquities, Lord, who could stand?

16

FOR A PERSON
OF POOR REPUTATION

Instrumental Prelude   "Amazing Grace"; "There's a Wideness in God's Mercy"

The Opening Sentences   God has shown us how much he loves us: it was while we were still sinners that Christ died for us! (Romans 5:8).

"Suppose one of you has a hundred sheep and loses one of them—what does he do? He leaves the ninety-nine sheep in the pasture and goes looking for the lost sheep until he finds it" (Luke 15:4).

Invocation Prayer

Lord God—thank You for the Gospel's assurance
that no person is too small for Your concern,
that no person is too sinful to be outside of Your love,
that no person is completely deserving of Your patience.

So in utter humility we bow before You. In gratitude
of heart, we praise You. In confidence, we trust
our beloved to You. O God, be merciful to us who
are sinners. Save us, through Jesus Christ our Lord.
Amen.

Hymn (*optional*)   "The Lord Is My Shepherd" (*solo,
song by congregation, organ interlude, or reading by
minister*)

Scripture Readings
From the Old Testament   Out of the depths I cry to
thee, O LORD! Lord, hear my voice! Let thy ears be
attentive to the voice of my supplications!

If thou, O LORD, shouldst mark iniquities, Lord, who
could stand? But there is forgiveness with thee, that
thou mayest be feared.

I wait for the LORD, my soul waits, and in his word I
hope; my soul waits for the LORD more than watchmen
for the morning, more than watchmen for the morning.

O Israel, hope in the LORD! For with the LORD there
is steadfast love, and with him is plenteous redemption.
And he will redeem Israel from all his iniquities (Psalms
130:1–8).

From the New Testament   For God loved the world so
much that he gave his only Son, so that everyone who
believes in him may not die but have eternal life (John
3:16).

Nor does the Father himself judge anyone. He has
given his Son the full right to judge, so that all will honor
the Son in the same way as they honor the Father. Who-

ever does not honor the Son does not honor the Father who sent him.

"I tell you the truth: whoever hears my words, and believes in him who sent me, has eternal life. He will not be judged, but has already passed from death to life" (John 5:22–24).

Come near to God, and he will come near to you. Wash your hands, sinners! Cleanse your hearts. . . . Humble yourselves before God, and he will lift you up. Do not speak against one another, my brothers. Whoever speaks against his brother, or judges him, speaks against the Law and judges it. If you judge the Law, then you are no longer a man who obeys the Law, but one who judges it. God is the only lawgiver and judge. He alone can save and destroy. Who do you think you are, to judge your fellow man? (James 4:8–12).

Meditation   "All Depend Upon Grace"

"As a father pities his children, so the LORD pities those who fear him" (Psalms 103:13).

God cares for the soul.   Whatever be our circumstance, the good news of the Gospel is: God cares for us—the least and the last, the good and the bad. We are never beyond the reaches of His compassionate concern.

It is perfectly clear, if one studies the Bible, that all of us are completely dependent upon God's grace. That is true in life. No life could exist apart from the grace of God. It is even more recognizable at the time of death. When we are stripped of all our physical reliances and left without our social, monetary, or authoritarian supports, how utterly we are dependent upon God. Not by merit, but by grace are we provided for in the future.

None of us has deserved or earned eternal life for "all have sinned and fall short of the glory of God" (Romans 3:23). God has reached out His love while we were yet sinners. Without His love overruling our tendencies and perversions, we all would come at last to the awful harvest of our perversity and sin. Richard Baxter, the Puritan writer, once watched a criminal being taken to the galley for hanging. "There go I," he whispered, "save for the grace of God."

The future is not for our determination or judgment. This one, like all of us in the hour of death, is cast upon the mercy and love of God. By God's choice and decisive action, He has willed and planned for our destiny. God has the first and last word in the matter. He is the Alpha and the Omega. So in humility and trust, we commit the future to Him, confident in love and righteousness.

Poem (*optional*)

The Sheepfold

Poor little black sheep that strayed away,
  Lost in the wind and the rain—
And the Shepherd He said, "O hireling,
  Go find my sheep again."

And the hireling said, "O Shepherd,
  That sheep is black and bad,"
But the Shepherd He smiled, like that little black sheep
  Was the only lamb He had.

And the Shepherd went out in the darkness
  Where the night was cold and bleak,

And that little black sheep, He found it,
  And laid it against His cheek.

And the hireling frowned, "O Shepherd,
  Don't bring that sheep to me!"
But the Shepherd He smiled, and He held it close,
  And . . . that little black sheep . . . was . . . me! [29]

Pastoral Prayer   Almighty and everlasting God, who
art a very present help in trouble; when our heart is
overwhelmed our refuge is in Thee. Thou art the
Father of our Lord Jesus Christ, the same yesterday,
today, and for ever, and of Thy love there is no end.
Grant, we pray, that Thy presence shall be more real
to us than our sorrow, and that we may have such
faith in Thee that we shall experience mercy, repent-
ance, and peace.

Our Heavenly Father, to us who live, enrich us in
those qualities over which death has no dominion; and
bring us at last, with Thy saints, to that glorious in-
heritance promised for Thy faithful children, through
Jesus Christ our Lord. *Amen.*

Hymn (*optional*)   "Day by Day" (*solo, song by congregation, organ interlude, or reading by minister*)

Postlude   "O Divine Redeemer"; "Have Thine Own
Way"

Her children rise up and call her blessed.

17

FOR AN OLDER MOTHER

Instrumental Prelude   "Now Thank We All Our God";
"Immortal, Invisible, God Only Wise"

The Opening Sentences   Precious in the sight of the
Lord is the death of his saints (Psalms 116:15). . . .
the Lord gave, and the Lord has taken away; blessed
be the name of the Lord (Job 1:21). There shall be
continuous day (it is known to the Lord), not day and
not night, for at evening time there shall be light
(Zechariah 14:7).

Invocation Prayer   Father God, eternal Lord of life
and death, we acknowledge Thee in all our ways and
in all the events which come to us. All our deep springs
are in Thee. May we feel Thee near now and know Thy
mercy is upholding us. In sorrow of heart, yet in quietness and confidence, we have gathered here to express
appreciation for one who is very near and dear, and to
find comfort in Thy presence, through Jesus Christ our
Lord, who taught us to pray (*in unison*):

> Our Father, who art in heaven,
> Hallowed be Thy name.

Thy kingdom come,
Thy will be done
On earth as it is in heaven.
Give us this day our daily bread;
And forgive us our debts,
As we forgive our debtors.
And lead us not into temptation,
But deliver us from evil;
For thine is the kingdom, and the power,
And the glory, forever. *Amen.*

Hymn (*optional*) "Motherhood, Sublime, Eternal" (*solo, song by congregation, organ interlude, or reading by minister*)

Scripture Readings
From the Old Testament It is good to give thanks to the LORD, to sing praises to thy name, O Most High; to declare thy steadfast love in the morning, and thy faithfulness by night. . . . For thou, O LORD, hast made me glad by thy work; at the works of thy hands I sing for joy. . . . The righteous flourish like the palm tree, and grow like a cedar in Lebanon. They are planted in the house of the LORD, they flourish in the courts of our God. They still bring forth fruit in old age . . . (Psalms 92:1–14).

A good wife who can find? She is far more precious than jewels. The heart of her husband trusts in her, and he will have no lack of gain. She does him good, and not harm, all the days of her life. . . . She opens her hand to the poor, and reaches out her hands to the needy. . . . Strength and dignity are her clothing, and she laughs at the time to come. She opens her mouth with wisdom, and the teaching of kindness is on her tongue. She looks well to the ways of her household, and does not eat the bread of idleness. Her children rise up and call her blessed; her husband also, and he praises her: "Many women have done excellently, but you surpass them all." Charm is deceitful, and beauty is vain, but a woman who fears the LORD is to be praised. Give her of the fruit of her hands, and let her works praise her in the gates (Proverbs 31:10–31).

From the New Testament "Then the King will say to the people on his right: 'You who are blessed by my Father: come! Come and receive the kingdom which has been prepared for you ever since the creation of the world. I was hungry and you fed me, thirsty and you gave me drink; I was a stranger and you received me in your homes, naked and you clothed me; I was sick and you took care of me, in prison and you visited me.' The righteous will then answer him: 'When, Lord, did we ever see you hungry and feed you, or thirsty and give you drink? When did we ever see you a stranger and welcome you in our homes, or naked and clothe you? When did we see you sick or in prison, and visit you?' The King will answer back, 'I tell you, indeed, whenever you did this for one of the least important of these brothers of mine, you did it for me!' " (Matthew 25:34–40).

Never again will they hunger or thirst; neither sun nor any scorching heat will burn them; for the Lamb, who is in the center of the throne, will be their shepherd, and guide them to springs of living water; and God will wipe away every tear from their eyes" (Revelation 7:16, 17).

The world and everything in it that men desire is passing away; but he who does what God wants lives for ever (1 John 2:17).

Poems (*optional*)

The Bravest Battle

The bravest battle that ever was fought
    Shall I tell you where and when?
On the maps of the world you will find it not
    'Twas fought by the mothers of men.

Nay, not with cannon, or battle-shot
    With sword, or nobler pen;
Nay, not with eloquent word or thought
    From mouths of wonderful men.

But deep in a welled-up woman's heart
    A woman who would not yield,
But bravely, silently bore her part—
    Lo! there is that battlefield!

No marshalling troop, no bivouac song—
    No banners to gleam and wave!
But, oh! these battles, they last so long—
    From babyhood to the grave!

Yet faithful still as a bridge of stars
    She fights in her walled-up town.
Fights on, and on, in her endless wars,
    Then, silent, unseen, goes down!

Oh, ye, with banners and battle-shot,
    With soldiers to shout and praise,
I tell you the kingliest victories fought
    Are fought in these silent ways.

Oh, spotless woman, in a world of shame
    With splendid and silent scorn,

Go back to God as pure as you came
    The queenliest warrior born.[30]

The Watcher

She always leaned to watch for us,
    Anxious if we were late,
In winter by the window,
    In summer by the gate;

And though we mocked her tenderly,
    Who had such foolish care,
The long way home would seem more safe
    Because she waited there.

Her thoughts were all so full of us,
    She never could forget!
And so I think that where she is
    She must be watching yet,

Waiting till we come home to her,
    Anxious if we are late—
Watching from Heaven's window,
    Leaning from Heaven's gate.[31]

Meditation   "A Mother's Honor"

"Honor your father and your mother, that your days may be long in the land which the LORD your God gives you" (Exodus 20:12).

White hair is a crown of glory and is seen most among the godly (Proverbs 16:31, Living Bible).

Today we are gathered here to honor and give respect to one who through long years has been found in the way of righteousness. Frequently in the Bible we find reference to the aged godly men and women such as Samuel, Job, Simeon, Anna, John the Beloved.

They were reverenced with esteem; they were respected. Their white hair, indicating advanced age, was a sign of heavenly favor and the fulfillment of the promise, "With long life I will satisfy him, and show him my salvation" (Psalms 91:16). The fading hair, the dimmed, drooping eyes, the furrowed face, the bent back, the gnarled hand allude to the long struggle. They depict the veteran who has "fought the good fight and kept the faith."

Friends testify to this mother's self-sacrificing toil, spiritual maturity, and service to others. The children have attached an obligation to the fourth commandment, "Honor your father and mother" (this is the first commandment with a promise), "that it may be well with you and that you may live long on the earth" (Ephesians 6:2, 3).

For these and other reasons ancient King Solomon assures us that "white hair is a crown of glory." However, note the qualifying phrase in the King James Version, which reads, ". . . if it be found in the way of righteousness." The Revised Standard Version reads, ". . . if it is gained in a righteous life," which merely means, not all who are aged are found in the way of righteousness.

Many a gray and lined person has lived without God and in total indifference to the will of God. Some have no positive contribution to righteousness at all. If vice is bad in youth, how progressively worse it is in old age. If evil becomes entrenched by habits of long years, then the influence and example of such a one is detrimental. The value of counsel from such for the oncoming generation is worthless. Old age may reflect ingratitude, selfishness, cruel paganism, and stark secularism. No honor or respect is to be given such.

How different is the aged mother found in the way of righteousness! To such God is known as a friend. There human love prevails. The evidence of the years becomes apparent and is recognized. She is revered and respected. Children seek her counsel on faith and life. Her gentle and loving spirit makes its silent witness in the heart of all who cross her path. There is comfort and hope for that one when the shadows lengthen and death comes.

So, dear family, proudly honor your mother. Rejoice, for the aged white head is "a crown of glory" for "it has been gained in a righteous life."

Pastoral Prayer Heavenly Father: there is much to be thankful for today. This mother lived long enough to be known by her children and grandchildren, sharing her faith, wisdom, values and character—a measureless heritage. Grant to her family, dear Lord, the knowledge and responsibility to use humbly that which has been bequeathed to them.

Merciful Lord, remove the guilt we feel today for not doing more than we have and for bringing sadness to our mothers. Flood our souls just now with an assurance of divine forgiveness. Right the wrongs in our lives by Thy Holy Spirit, and help us so to live that we may never bring disgrace to our mothers.

We thank Thee, our Father, for the promised eternal home; for the promise to be our constant heavenly parent; and for the promise that though "weeping may tarry for the night . . . joy comes with the morning" (Psalms 30:5). In Jesus' name. *Amen.*

Hymn (*optional*)   "All Creatures of Our God and King" (*solo, song by congregation, organ interlude, or reading by minister*)

Benediction   God has raised from the dead our Lord Jesus, who is the Great Shepherd of the sheep because of his death, by which the eternal covenant is sealed. May the God of peace provide you with every good thing you need in order to do his will, and may he, through Jesus Christ, do in us what pleases him. And to Christ be the glory for ever and ever! Amen (Hebrews 13:20, 21).

Postlude   "Postlude" (Haydn); "Blest Be the Tie That Binds"

I have run the full distance. I have kept the faith.

18

FOR AN AGED FATHER

Instrumental Prelude   "O God, Our Help in Ages Past"; "Rock of Ages"

The Opening Sentence   He who dwells in the shelter of the Most High, who abides in the shadow of the

Almighty, will say to the LORD, "My refuge and my fortress; my God, in whom I trust" (Psalms 91:1, 2).

Invocation Prayer   Everliving God, before whose face pass the generations of men, whose mercies are from everlasting to everlasting, Thou hast taught that in quietness and confidence shall be our strength; by the power of the Spirit, lift us to Thy presence where we may be still and know that Thou art God through Jesus Christ the Lord. *Amen.*

Scripture Readings
From the Old Testament   Have you not known? Have you not heard? The LORD is the everlasting God, the Creator of the ends of the earth. He does not faint or grow weary, his understanding is unsearchable. He gives power to the faint, and to him who has no might he increases strength. Even youths shall faint and be weary, and young men shall fall exhausted; but they who wait for the LORD shall renew their strength, they shall mount up with wings like eagles, they shall run and not be weary, they shall walk and not faint (Isaiah 40:28–31).

Because you have made the LORD your refuge, the Most High your habitation, no evil shall befall you, no scourge come near your tent. For he will give his angels charge of you to guard you in all your ways. On their hands they will bear you up, lest you dash your foot against a stone. . . . Because he cleaves to me in love, I will deliver him; I will protect him, because he knows my name. When he calls to me, I will answer him; I will be with him in trouble, I will rescue him and honor him. With long life I will satisfy him, and show him my salvation (Psalms 91:9–16).

Lord, thou hast been our dwelling place in all generations. Before the mountains were brought forth, or ever thou hadst formed the earth and the world, from everlasting to everlasting thou art God. Thou turnest man back to the dust, and sayest, "Turn back, O children of men!" For a thousand years in thy sight are but as yesterday when it is past, or as a watch in the night. Thou dost sweep men away; they are like a dream, like grass which is renewed in the morning: in the morning it flourishes and is renewed; in the evening it fades and withers. . . . Satisfy us in the morning with thy steadfast love, that we may rejoice and be glad all our days. Make us glad as many days as thou has afflicted us, and as many years as we have seen evil. Let thy work be manifest to thy servants, and thy glorious power to their children. Let the favor of the LORD our God be upon us, and establish thou the work of our hands upon us, yea, the work of our hands establish thou it (Psalms 90:1–17).

From the New Testament . . . the time is here for me to leave this life. I have done my best in the race, I have run the full distance, I have kept the faith. And now the prize of victory is waiting for me, the crown of righteousness which the Lord, the righteous Judge, will give me on that Day—and not only to me, but to all those who wait with love for him to appear (2 Timothy 4:6–8).

One of the elders asked me, "Who are those people dressed in white robes, and where do they come from?"

"I don't know, sir. You do," I answered. He said to me: "These are the people who have come safely through the great persecution. They washed their robes and made them white with the blood of the Lamb. That is why they stand before God's throne and serve him day and night in his temple. He who sits on the throne will protect them with his presence. Never again will they hunger or thirst; neither sun nor any scorching heat will burn them; for the Lamb, who is in the center of the throne, will be their shepherd, and guide them to springs of living water; and God will wipe away every tear from their eyes" (Revelation 7:13–17).

Poems (*optional*)

Heaven at Last

Angel voices sweetly singing
Echoes through the blue dome ringing,
News of wondrous gladness bringing;
    Ah, 'tis heaven at last!

On the jasper threshold standing,
Like a pilgrim safely landing;
See, the strange bright scene expanding,
    Ah, 'tis heaven at last!

Sin forever left behind us,
Earthly visions cease to blind us,
Earthly fetters cease to bind us,
    Ah, 'tis heaven at last!

Not a teardrop ever falleth,
Not a pleasure ever palleth,
Song to song forever calleth;
    Ah, 'tis heaven at last!

Christ Himself the living splendor,
Christ the sunlight mild and tender;
Praises to the Lamb we render,
    Ah, 'tis heaven at last! [32]

Rest

Rest—with each vision of the future blended
    Comes that bright hope, so soothing and so dear,
All the long journey past, the conflict ended,
    Rest—but not here!

Not here! While war's alarm is ever sounding
    While half the promised land is unpossessed,
On the red battle-plain, with foes surrounding.
    Who dares to rest?

Not here! When autumn's sun is brightly shining,
    Yet storm-clouds gather in the darkening west,
On the ripe corn-fields, till the sun's declining,
    Who thinks of rest?

Not here, but yonder—where in peace forever
    The faithful servants with their Lord are blest
Where friends depart, and foes shall enter never—
    There we shall rest.

Yes; and that prospect now the heart sustaineth
    Lightly each burden and each toil to bear;
For us the promise holds, the rest "remaineth,"
    Not here—but there.[33]

Pastoral Prayer   O Lord, how destitute we would be
this day, without the good news of love at the heart of
all. How melancholy and forlorn we would be this day,
had we never heard of Jesus, who said, "Peace I leave
with you . . ." (John 14:27). How hopeless and

pathetic our outlook if it were not for the resurrection faith. Thanks be to Thee, O God, for the hope and life eternal that Jesus Christ has brought to light. Help us to lift up our heads in faith; to put a smile of joy upon the face; to walk on tiptoe because Thou art great.

We thank Thee, O God, for the life of this good father, for his dedication, his unselfishness, his sense of humor, his good judgment, and all qualities of character that have endeared him to family and friends.

Father of mercy, support these friends with the church's fellowship. Bind up their wounds of the heart by Thy love. Remove feelings of remorse and resentment with forgiveness.

Help us to know how fragile life is, so that we may invest our time and energy serving Thy will with constancy until our summons comes. Then may we be united with Thy blessed ones through Jesus Christ. *Amen.*

Hymn (*optional*) "For All the Saints, Who From Their Labors Rest" (*solo, song by congregation, organ interlude, or reading by minister*)

Meditation "Once Hopelessness . . . But Now, Hope!"

Suppose when you lost a dear one, and followed the slow procession to the grave, you had never heard of Jesus' Resurrection? How desolate would be the world and inconsolable your grief, if you had never heard of Jesus' forgiving sins and conquering death by transcending its awful grip! Melancholy and hopelessness would be the mood of this moment, if God had not shattered the midnight of darkness by the light of an empty tomb. If there is nothing beyond the sunset and the dark, if death is a sleep from which there is no awakening, if the grave is the end of existence—then our pilgrimage here is rather purposeless, intolerably pathetic, with little incentive for goodness.

Gloriously, however, something has happened to give us hope for this day. "If for this life only we have hoped in Christ, we are of all men most to be pitied," said Paul. "But in fact Christ has been raised from the dead . . ." (1 Corinthians 15:19, 20). "But in fact . . . !" How assuring those words! Something has happened! Something tremendous has a foothold in this darkened scene that has changed the face of the world. Something about Christ's Resurrection has made us talk today of life not death.

Clement of Alexandria claimed: "Christ has turned all our sunsets into dawns." This is no exaggeration! It is not emotional hyperbole! It is not just religious fanaticism. It is a historic testimony that has removed the "sting of death," and changed forever the human prospect. Since that happening, the people of God have faced the last enemy with courage and faith. True believers have been able to endure the death of loved ones serenely, to face their own dying unshaken, without being undone.

Once death was the end and ruin of hope. "Sunset and evening star" was sheer tragedy. "Death," said Aristotle, "is a fearful thing, for it is the end." Once this was so.

But *now*. Now is Christ risen! Now death is ultimately defeated! Now the sunset gives promise of a resurrection dawn! Now you can meet this loss with hope! You can walk unshaken toward the night "when thy summons comes to join that innumerable caravan." Now you can "wrap the drapery of your couch about you and lie down to pleasant dreams." Because "Christ is risen from the dead." And "because I live," He said, "you will live also" (John 14:19).

> Ring out, wild bells, to the wild sky,
> Ring in the Christ that is to be.

Hymn (*optional*)   "Faith of Our Fathers" (*solo, song by congregation, organ interlude, or reading by minister*)

Benediction   May God, the source of hope, fill you with all joy and peace by means of your faith in him, so that your hope will continue to grow by the power of the Holy Spirit (Romans 15:13). *Amen.*

Postlude   "In His Love Abiding"; "Under His Wings"

"And the door will be open to him who knocks."

19

FOR A STRANGER

Instrumental Prelude   "Come Thou Almighty King"; "Largo" (Dvorak)

The Opening Sentences   The Lord is near to all who call upon him, to all who call upon him in truth. He fulfills the desire of all who fear him, he also hears their cry, and saves them (Psalms 145:18, 19). Ask, and you will receive; seek, and you will find; knock, and the door will be opened to you. For everyone who asks will receive, and he who seeks will find, and the door will be opened to him who knocks (Matthew 7:7, 8).

Invocation Prayer   O God, in whom we live and move and have our being, who has promised that those who are pure in heart shall see Thee, to whom no person is unknown; we bow reverently before Thee, knocking, seeking, asking· Only Thou can satisfy our deeper yearnings for peace and love, for fulfillment and eternal life, through Jesus Christ our Lord. *Amen.*

Scripture Readings
From the Old Testament   Whither shall I go from thy Spirit? Or whither shall I flee from thy presence? If I ascend to heaven, thou art there! If I make my bed in Sheol, thou art there! If I take the wings of the morning and dwell in the uttermost parts of the sea, even there thy hand shall lead me, and thy right hand shall hold me. If I say, "Let only darkness cover me, and the light about me be night," even the darkness is not dark to thee, the night is bright as the day; for darkness is as light with thee (Psalms 139:7–12).

From the New Testament   "Be ready for whatever comes, with your clothes fastened tight at the waist and your lamps lit, like servants who are waiting for their master to come back from a wedding feast. When he comes and knocks, they will open the door for him at once. How happy are those servants whose master finds them awake and ready! I tell you, he will fasten his belt, have them sit down, and wait on them. How happy are they if he finds them ready, even if he should come as late as midnight or even later! And remember this! If the man of the house knew the time when the thief would come, he would not let the thief break into his house. And you, too, be ready, because the Son of Man will come at an hour when you are not expecting him" (Luke 12:35–40).

For this reason, then, I fall on my knees before the Father, from whom every family in heaven and on earth receives its true name. I ask God, from the wealth of his glory, to give you power through his Spirit to be strong in your inner selves, and that Christ will make his home in your hearts, through faith. I pray that you may have your roots and foundations in love, and that you, together with all God's people, may have the power to understand how broad and long and high and deep is Christ's love. Yes, may you come to know his love— although it can never be fully known—and so be completely filled with the perfect fulness of God. To him who is able to do so much more than we can ever ask for, or even think of, by means of the power working in us: to God be the glory in the church and in Christ Jesus, for all time, for ever and ever! Amen (Ephesians 3:14–21).

Hymn (*optional*) "Sun of My Soul, Thou Saviour Dear" (*solo, song by congregation, organ interlude, or reading by minister*)

Meditation "The Bridge That Love Built"

Have you ever seen, or crossed over the Golden Gate Bridge? It is perhaps the monumental example of engineering skill linking San Francisco with the mainland.

Geologists tell us that the entire peninsula area is a geological fault, a portion of land that has been broken off from the mainland, perhaps precipitated by an earthquake thousands of years ago. The Golden Gate Bridge gives northern access to this uniquely beautiful city. Under the bridge passes the ocean traffic of the world seeking a friendly harbor. Over it pass thousands of travelers daily, returning to their homes after a day's work or journey.

I use the Golden Gate Bridge as an analogy of the implications of the Golden Text of the Bible, John 3:16, "God so loved the world that he gave his only Son, that whoever believes in him should not perish but have eternal life."

We in a sense have been broken apart from our Creator, and the homeland of our souls. We have been surrounded by troubled waters, alienated from God's complete, perfect will and His beautiful presence. God's love, in Jesus Christ, has opened up communication, reconciled us with our Maker, helped us escape being cut off, for now we have a bridge leading to eternal life. That bridge has spanned the chasm between man and God, earth and heaven, and has linked now with eternity. Praise God for this assurance. It is the balm of Gilead for healing the broken in heart. It is the highway to those lost in the darkness of doubt. It is the lifeline to save those at the end of their health. It is hope for the despairing. It is comfort for the bereaved. It is the glorious provision for those of faith whose earthly journey is complete. It is the bridge to heaven.

There are many people who deny wanting heaven with their minds, but affirm it with their hearts. When a social worker goes into a ghetto and is sickened by what he sees, clinches his fists and says, "These horrible places will have to go. Human beings must not live in misery and squalor," whether he realizes it or not, he is unconsciously projecting an inner hunger for a world minus hunger and filth. Heaven is that kind of condition: "They shall hunger no more."

Every time statesmen sit together to devise a solution to war, unconsciously they are projecting an inner hunger for a world minus bloodshed and death. Heaven is such a condition.

When a doctor or a scientist goes into his laboratory to seek a cure for cancer or heal disease, whether he realizes it or not, he is projecting an inner hunger for the perfection that heaven promises.

This is the kind of life the bridge leads to—and more, for ". . . no eye has seen, nor ear heard, nor the heart of man conceived, what God has prepared for those who love him" (1 Corinthians 2:9).

Therefore, do not be downhearted. Rather rejoice in the Lord.

Pastoral Prayer Our Father God, upon these over whom the darkness of death hangs, let come the consoling whispering of Thy comforter. In their loneliness be their companion. Be to them hope and life and love. Out of the desolation of loss rear the structures of hope. Grant that each troubled heart may find in Thy promises and presence, the rest it needs. Teach us all to listen to Him who brings that peace which is beyond understanding. May the experience of sharing Him who bears our sorrows and carries our afflictions bring strength to our friends. In His fellowship, keep them until the morn eternal dawns, and all the shadows have vanished, and we see Thee face-to-face, through Jesus Christ the Lord. *Amen.*

Hymn(*optional*) "I'm a Pilgrim"   (*solo, song by congregation, organ interlude, or reading by minister*)

Benediction   May God, the source of hope, fill you with all joy and peace by means of your faith in him, so that your hope will continue to grow by the power of the Holy Spirit (Romans 15:13). *Amen.*

Postlude   "My Heart Is Filled With Longing" (Bach)

Precious in the sight of the LORD *is the death of his saints.*

20

FOR AN OUTSTANDING CHRISTIAN

Instrumental Prelude   "Blest Are the Departed" (Spohr); "For All the Saints Who From Their Labor Rest"

The Opening Sentences   Then I heard a voice from heaven saying: "Write this: Happy are the dead who from now on die in the service of the Lord!" "Certainly so," answers the Spirit. "They will enjoy rest from their hard work; for they take with them the results of their service" (Revelation 14:13).

For we know that when this tent we live in—our body here on earth—is torn down, God will have a house in heaven for us to live in, a home he himself made, which will last forever (2 Corinthians 5:1).

Invocation Prayer   Lord, Thou has been our dwelling place in all generations. Before the mountains were brought forth, or ever thou hadst formed the earth and the world, from everlasting to everlasting thou art God (Psalms 90:1, 2). Help us to be still and know that Thou art God, through Jesus Christ, our Lord. *Amen.*

Hymn (*optional*)   "Ten Thousand Times Ten Thousand" (*solo, song by congregation, organ interlude, or reading by minister*)

Scripture Readings
From the Old Testament   Blessed is the man who walks not in the counsel of the wicked, nor stands in the way of sinners, nor sits in the seat of scoffers; but his delight is in the law of the LORD, and on his law he meditates day and night. He is like a tree planted by streams of water, that yields its fruit in its season, and its leaf does not wither. In all that he does, he prospers.

The wicked are not so, but are like chaff which the wind drives away. Therefore the wicked will not stand in the judgment, nor sinners in the congregation of the righteous; for the LORD knows the way of the righteous, but the way of the wicked will perish (Psalm 1).

Precious in the sight of the LORD is the death of his saints. . . . I will offer to thee the sacrifice of thanksgiving and call on the name of the LORD. I will pay my vows to the LORD in the presence of all his people (Psalms 116:15–18).

From the New Testament   "It will be like a man who was about to leave home on a trip: he called his servants and put them in charge of his property. He gave to each one according to his ability: to one he gave five thousand dollars, to the other two thousand dollars, and to the other one thousand dollars. Then he left on his trip. The servant who had received five thousand dollars went at once and invested his money and earned another five thousand dollars. In the same way the servant who received two thousand dollars earned another two thousand dollars. But the servant who received one thousand dollars went off, dug a hole in the ground, and hid his master's money.

"After a long time the master of those servants came back and settled accounts with them. The servant who had received five thousand dollars came in and handed over the other five thousand dollars. 'You gave me five thousand dollars, sir,' he said. 'Look! Here are another five thousands dollars that I have earned.' 'Well done, good and faithful servant!' said his master. 'You have been faithful in managing small amounts, so I will put you in charge of large amounts. Come on in, and share my happiness!' Then the servant who had been given two thousand dollars came in and said, 'You gave me two thousand dollars, sir. Look! Here are another two thousand dollars that I have earned.' 'Well done, good and faithful servant!' said his master. 'You have been faithful in managing small amounts, so I will put you in charge of large amounts. Come on in and share my happiness!' " (Matthew 25:14–23).

"Then the King will say to the people on his right: 'You who are blessed by my Father: Come! Come and receive the kingdom which has been prepared for you ever since the creation of the world. I was hungry and you fed me, thirsty and you gave me drink; I was a stranger and you received me in your homes, naked and you clothed me; I was sick and you took care of me, in prison and you visited me.' The righteous will then answer him: 'When, Lord, did we ever see you hungry and feed you, or thirsty and give you drink? When did we ever see you a stranger and welcome you in our homes, or naked and clothe you? When did we ever see you sick or in prison and visit you?' The King will answer back, 'I tell you, indeed, whenever you did this for one of the least important of these brothers of mine, you did it for me!' " (Matthew 25:34–40).

See how much the Father has loved us! His love is so great that we are called God's children—and so, in fact, we are. This is why the world does not know us: it has not known God. My dear friends, we are now God's children, but it is not yet clear what we shall become. But this we know: when Christ appears, we shall become like him, because we shall see him as he really is (1 John 3:1, 2).

Poems (*optional*)

> My soul is bound for gloryland;
>   No pain, nor grief, nor loss;
> Nor weary tramp through desert sand,
>   Nor poverty, nor cross,
> Nor foiled desires, nor sin, nor death,
>   Nor Satan's piercing dart
> Can quench the spirit-kindled faith
>   Within my trusting heart.

My soul is bound for gloryland;
   I'll lay my burden down
And from my Savior's nail-scarred hand
   Receive the promised crown,
His love shall wipe all tears away;
   I'll know as I am known.
He taught my tested faith to pray:
   "Thy will, not mine be done."

Amen.[34]

There is no death
Our loved ones fall
And pass away.
They only await
The Savior's call;
To reign in His
Eternal Day.[35]

The Final Quest

I shall go forth some day
Forgetting the foolishness of song and rhyming,
And slowly travel life's wood until twilight
Whispers: "This is the end of earth's journey:
Your pathway
Is now up, past the stars;
Keep on climbing." [36]

Pastoral Prayer   Father God, who has been our dwelling place in all generations from everlasting to everlasting, who has given to us life and the opportunity to serve in love; we bless Thy Holy Name.

We thank Thee for the revelation of Thyself in the lives of others, including the one we have come to honor today. For his love of Jesus Christ and the church, for his radiant and kind spirit, for his wisdom and courage,

for his unselfish deeds and gentle manner, we thank
Thee, O God. Inspired by his example in courtesy, service, and Christian dedication, help us, O God, to walk
in his footsteps as we follow our Master, Jesus Christ.

By Thy providence, Thou hast called him to be with
Thee in the larger life beyond this life. We are comforted by the assurance that death, which has brought
us sorrow, has meant release and peace to our loved
one.

Help us, as we contemplate the qualities of righteousness seen in our friend, to catch the challenge of his life
and to prepare ourselves so that in that day when we
shall be called, we may hear the words, "Well done,
thou good and faithful servant . . . enter into the joy
of thy Lord." So may it be, in Christ's name. *Amen*.[37]

Meditation   "The Higher Ground"

Have you ever driven to the top of Pike's Peak in
Colorado? There are a series of hairpin curves which
lift one up stage by stage to the lofty peak towering
high above the Colorado prairie and surrounding mountains. As one progresses up the steep grades, frequently
he can look back to where he has been and at the same
time see the "rungs in the ladder" ahead and beyond to
the ultimate peak.

So life is a steady struggle upward toward the lofty
peak of God's perfection. "You, therefore, must be
perfect as your heavenly Father is perfect," said Jesus
(Matthew 5:48). As our comprehension of life ex-
pands and we rise in God-consciousness, we climb the
ladder of God's spirit.

The one whom we have met to honor has climbed
high in the earthly pilgrimage toward spiritual maturity.

He has been an inspiration for he has lived above the pollution of the valley, breathing the fresh air of Christ's spirit, in fellowship with other followers of the Christ. Even now he continues to grow and develop in soul, for, in my opinion, we are the same souls after death as we are before the death of our physical homes.

Paul in 2 Corinthians 12:4 describes a man "caught up into a third heaven" and heard unspeakable words "which man may not utter." Paul had a glimpse of a developed soul that was so glorious he could find no words to describe it. And who knows how many heavens beyond the third there may be in our Father's house, or how many rooms that we may enter and leave before we arrive in the blessed pure perfection of God's presence.

Or, change the figure if you wish. Think of life as advancement through school. With this view, the world is an elementary school in which the first lessons of truth, love, and beauty are learned. It is the antechamber to the vast university of eternity in which there are many schools and colleges for those who have reached different degrees of faith and holiness. Eternal life is the extension of the courses in the spirit we have taken here. A person will carry over into the world on the other side of death the qualities which he had developed here. Death will not arrest one's progress. Those inclined toward Godlikeness will rise closer to Him. "God Himself shall be with them." This will be heavenly. It will be the heaven of heavens. Those who have not matured to love the things of God nor to like what Christ liked shall be miserable indeed, and will drift farther away from God's house into "outer darkness."

John's Revelation 21:1 reads, "Then I saw a new

heaven and a new earth; for the first heaven and the first earth had passed away." This refers to the consummation of the ages. He meant, it seems to me, that one age or stage shall pass away in order for the higher to emerge, until in the end the perfection of a "new heaven" is realized. It is unspeakable and unimaginable glory which "eye has not seen, nor ear heard, neither has it entered into the heart of man. . . ." This is the final goal of every human life, and it is the bliss we call *heaven*.

Our friend is on his way. He inspires us on, as does the poet who wrote "Higher Ground."

Hymn (*optional*)   "Higher Ground" (*solo, song by congregation, organ interlude, or reading by minister*)

Benediction   May the Lord himself, who is our source of peace, give you peace at all times and in every way. The Lord be with you all (2 Thessalonians 3:16). *Amen.*

Postlude   "Hallelujah Chorus" (Handel)

*God will bring with Jesus those who have
died believing in him.*

21

FOR A NOMINAL CHURCH MEMBER

Instrumental Prelude   "Beneath the Cross of Jesus"

The Opening Sentences   None of us lives for himself
only, none of us dies for himself only; if we live, it is
for the Lord that we live, and if we die, it is for the
Lord that we die. Whether we live or die, then, we
belong to the Lord. For Christ died and rose to life in
order to be the Lord of the living and of the dead
(Romans 14:7–9).

Invocation Prayer   Source of all life, God of all
creation before and after death, Father of our spirits
beyond whose love we never are able to go; we acknowledge Thee in all our ways, and in all the events
which befall us. In sorrow, yet in quietness and confidence, we have gathered here for these solemn expres-
sions of love and faith. In sadness as in joy, in loss as in
gain, in death as in life, we worship Thee as Loving
God, known in Jesus Christ. *Amen.*

Hymn (*optional*)   "If With All Your Hearts" (*solo or
organ interlude*)

Scripture Readings

From the Old Testament   O LORD, who shall sojourn in thy tent? Who shall dwell on thy holy hill? He who walks blamelessly, and does what is right, and speaks truth from his heart; who does not slander with his tongue, and does no evil to his friend, nor takes up a reproach against his neighbor; in whose eyes a reprobate is despised, but who honors those who fear the Lord. . . . He who does these things shall never be moved (Psalms 15:1–5).

I love the LORD, because he has heard my voice and my supplications. Because he inclined his ear to me, therefore I will call on him as long as I live. The snares of death encompassed me; the pangs of Sheol laid hold on me; I suffered distress and anguish. Then I called on the name of the LORD: "O LORD, I beseech thee, save my life!"

Gracious is the LORD, and righteous; our God is merciful. The LORD preserves the simple; when I was brought low, he saved me. Return, O my soul, to your rest; for the Lord has dealt bountifully with you.

For thou hast delivered my soul from death, my eyes from tears, my feet from stumbling. . . . What shall I render to the LORD for all his bounty to me? I will lift up the cup of salvation and call on the name of the LORD. I will pay my vows to the LORD in thy presence of all his people (Psalms 116:1–8, 12–14).

From the New Testament   Brothers, we want you to know the truth about those who have died, so that you will not be sad, as are those who have no hope. We believe that Jesus died and rose again; so we believe that God will bring with Jesus those who have died believing in him (1 Thessalonians 4:13, 14).

To have faith is to be sure of the things we hope for, to be certain of the things we cannot see. It was by their faith that the men of ancient times won God's approval. It is by faith that we understand that the universe was created by God's word, so that what can be seen was made out of what cannot be seen. It was faith that made Abel offer to God a better sacrifice than Cain's. Through his faith he won God's approval as a righteous man, for God himself approved his gifts. By means of his faith Abel still speaks, even though he is dead. It was faith that kept Enoch from dying. Instead, he was taken up to God, and nobody could find him, because God had taken him up. The scripture says that before Enoch was taken up he had pleased God. No man can please God without faith. For he who comes to God must have faith that God exists and rewards those who seek him.

It was faith that made Noah hear God's warnings about things in the future that he could not see. He obeyed God, and built an ark in which he and his family were saved. In this way he condemned the world, and received from God the righteousness that comes by faith. It was faith that made Abraham obey when God called him, and go out to a country which God had promised to give him. He left his own country without knowing where he was going. By faith he lived in the country that God had promised him, as though he were a foreigner. He lived in tents with Isaac and Jacob, who had received the same promise from God. For Abraham was waiting for the city which God has designed and built, the city with permanent foundations (Hebrews 11:1–10).

We, however, are citizens of heaven, and we eagerly wait for our Savior to come from heaven, the Lord Jesus Christ. He will change our weak mortal bodies and make them like his own glorious body, using that power by which he is able to bring all things under his rule (Philippians 3:20, 21).

Poems (*optional*)

Celestial Souls

I like to think of Death,
not as a thing to fear
but an ascension, a lifting up,
releasing from this flesh
and earthly sphere
to planes where souls commune
with no more care
and share the glory
of God's Heavenly Dawn.[38]

A Silvery Light for Every Cloud

For every cloud, a silvery light,
    God wills it so.
For every vale a shining height,
A glorious morn for every night,
    And birth for labor's throe.

For snow's white wing, a verdant field;
    A gain for loss,
For buried seed the harvest yield;
For pain a strength, a joy revealed,
    A crown for every cross.[39]

How Beautiful to Be With God

How beautiful to be with God,
   When earth is fading like a dream,
And from this mist-encircled shore
   We launch upon the unknown stream.

No doubt, no fear, no anxious care,
   But comforted by staff and rod,
In the faith-brightened hour of Death
   How beautiful to be with God.

Then let it fade, this dream of earth,
   When I have done my life work here,
Or long, or short, as seemeth best—
   What matters so God's Will appear.

I will not fear to launch my bark,
   Upon the darkly rolling flood,
'Tis but to pierce the mist—and then
   How beautiful to be with God.[40]

Pastoral Prayer   Father God, the parent and comforter of Thy children, we pray for Thy sustaining grace to support those who mourn at this time. We thank Thee for the life of _____, whose qualities of character, good works, and personal relationships have endeared him to those gathered here.

We thank Thee, our Father, for the assurance in Jesus that death is not the destruction but the expansion of life; that it opens the way to new opportunities and forms of worship and service, maturity and joy; that death cannot take us out of Thy fatherly care nor separate us from Thy love. We do not know the details for we cannot see, but we are assured by faith that we never leave Thy house. We are the children of Thy eternal love, and underneath are the everlasting arms. Help us, Lord, even amid our distress, to affirm this faith and love, then shall we find Thy peace which passes all understanding, and even the bereavement which now darkens our homes will not break our trust in Jesus Christ. *Amen.*

Hymn (*optional*) "In the Cross of Christ I Glory" (*solo, song by congregation, organ interlude or reading by minister*)

Meditation "Each to His Own Place"

What happens to our loved ones, and others, when death occurs? What became of the disciples and the saints of the ages after death?

It is probably impossible to locate specific geographic regions on a cosmic map. There are two short verses in the New Testament that give intimations.

Recall Judas Iscariot of whom it is recorded in Acts 1:25 that he turned aside from the disciples "to go to his own place." The Bible offers no theories to explain his betrayal of Jesus at the Last Supper. All we have is his final obituary: "He went to his own place." He made an irrevocable decision that took him away from his Master's influence. With twisted thoughts and perverted reasoning, he sought and found his own level. It was the logical ending of his distorted values. This was his own place—the hell of being himself.

In striking contrast to the other disciples that same night, Jesus said, "I go to prepare a place for you . . . that where I am, you may be also" (John 14:2, 3).

They were no saints. Frequently they were quarrelsome, dull, unreliable, rebellious, notably Peter who denied the Lord three times—not a very good track record. Thomas displayed skepticism and unbelief. Yet none severed himself from the Master's influence. Though they were crushed on Good Friday, the group did not dissolve.

Jesus' words were their hope and comfort, "Where I am, there you will be." Where the place was, or what it would be like, He did not say. It was enough that there was a future for them that was good—a future because Christ had a future—good because Jesus would prepare it. The disciples' hope was bound up entirely with the future of Jesus Christ, as is ours. We shall by Christ's power and lure escape from ourselves and share the victory over sin and death. We are not left to prepare our own place. Jesus has prepared it. He offers to share the place if we are prepared to live in it.

So our business, dear friends, is to become prepared spiritually for Christ's place.

So live, that when thy summons comes to join
    The innumerable caravan, which moves
To that mysterious realm, where each shall take
    His chamber in the silent halls of death,
Thou go not, like a quarry-slave at night,
    Scourged to his dungeon, but, sustained and soothed
By an unfaltering trust, approach thy grave
    Like one who wraps the drapery of his couch
About him and lies down to pleasant dreams.[41]

Benediction But after you have suffered for a little while, the God of all grace, who calls you to share his eternal glory in union with Christ, will himself perfect you, and give you firmness, strength, and a sure foundation. To him be the power for ever! Amen (1 Peter 5:10, 11).

Postlude "One Sweet Solemn Thought"

The last enemy to be defeated will be death.

22

FOR A PERSON OF ADVANCED AGE

Instrumental Prelude "In the Cross of Christ I Glory"; "I Know My Redeemer Lives"

The Opening Sentences Jesus said: ". . . I am the resurrection and the life. Whoever believes in me will live, even though he dies; and whoever lives and believes in me will never die" (John 11:25, 26).

Invocation Prayer God of eternity, who has planted in our hearts the faith and hope which looks beyond our mortal life to another—even heavenly—abode; in the abundance of grace strengthen these friends in their sorrow. Enable them to look beyond the sadness of this hour, to see the bright shining light of immortality, which Jesus Christ brought to life, in His holy name. *Amen.*

Hymn (*optional*) "All Hail the Power of Jesus' Name" (*solo, song by congregation, organ interlude, or reading by minister*)

Scripture Readings

From the Old Testament   Lord, thou hast been our dwelling place in all generations. Before the mountains were brought forth, or ever thou hadst formed the earth and the world, from everlasting to everlasting thou art God. Thou turnest man back to the dust, and sayest, "Turn back, O children of men!" For a thousand years in thy sight are but as yesterday when it is past, or as a watch in the night. Thou dost sweep men away; they are like a dream, like grass which is renewed in the morning: in the morning it flourishes and is renewed; in the evening it fades and withers . . . The years of our life are threescore and ten, or even by reason of strength fourscore; yet their span is but toil and trouble; they are soon gone, and we fly away . . . So teach us to number our days that we may get a heart of wisdom . . . Satisfy us in the morning with thy steadfast love, that we may rejoice and be glad all our days . . . . Let thy work be manifest to thy servants, and thy glorious power to their children. Let the favor of the Lord our God be upon us, and establish thou the work of our hands upon us, yea, the work of our hands establish thou it (Psalms 90:1–6, 10, 12, 14, 16–17).

After the death of Moses the servant of the LORD, the LORD said to Joshua the son of Nun, Moses' minister, "Moses my servant is dead; now therefore arise, go over this Jordan, you and all this people, into the land which I am giving to them, to the people of Israel. . . . No man shall be able to stand before you all the days of your life; as I was with Moses, so I will be with you; I will not fail you or forsake you. . . . Only be strong

and very courageous, being careful to do according to
all the law which Moses my servant commanded you;
turn not from it to the right hand or to the left, that you
may have good success wherever you go. . . . Have I
not commanded you? Be strong and of good courage;
be not frightened, neither be dismayed; for the LORD
your God is with you wherever you go" (Joshua 1:1,
2, 5, 7, 9).

From the New Testament   But the truth is that Christ
has been raised from death, as the guarantee that those
who sleep in death will also be raised. For just as death
came by means of a man, in the same way the rising
from death comes by means of a man. For just as all
men die because of their union to Adam, in the same
way all will be raised to life because of their union to
Christ. But each one in his proper order: Christ, the
first of all; then those who belong to Christ, at the time
of his coming. Then the end will come; Christ will
overcome all spiritual rulers, authorities, and powers,
and hand over the Kingdom to God the Father. For
Christ must rule until God defeats all enemies and puts
them under his feet. The last enemy to be defeated will
be death. . . . Someone will ask, "How can the dead
be raised to life? What kind of body will they have?"
You fool! When you plant a seed in the ground it does
not sprout to life unless it dies. And what you plant in
the ground is a bare seed, perhaps a grain of wheat, or
of some other kind, not the full-bodied plant that will
grow up. God provides that seed with the body he
wishes; he gives each seed its own proper body. . . .
This is how it will be when the dead are raised to life.
When the body is buried it is mortal; when raised, it

will be immortal. When buried, it is . . . weak; when raised, it will be beautiful and strong. When buried, it is a physical body; when raised, it will be a spiritual body (1 Corinthians 15:20–26, 35–38, 42–44).

Let us give thanks to the God and Father of our Lord Jesus Christ! Because of his great mercy, he gave us new life by raising Jesus Christ from the dead. This fills us with a living hope, and so we look forward to possess the rich blessings that God keeps for his people. He keeps them for you in heaven, where they cannot decay or spoil or fade away. They are for you, who through faith are kept safe by God's power, as you wait for the salvation which is ready to be revealed at the end of time.

Be glad about this, even though it may now be necessary for you to be sad for a while because of the many kinds of trials you suffer. Their purpose is to prove that your faith is genuine. Even gold, which can be destroyed, is tested by fire; and so your faith, which is much more precious than gold, must also be tested, that it may endure. Then you will receive praise and glory and honor on the Day when Jesus Christ is revealed. You love him, although you have not seen him; you believe in him, although you do not now see him; and so you rejoice with a great and glorious joy, which words cannot express, because you are receiving the purpose of your faith, the salvation of your souls (1 Peter 1:3–9).

Pastoral Prayer O Thou, Eternal Spirit, whom our forefathers trusted, and who brought them to the city eternal; we bow in thankfulness for the faith and good works of the one in whose memory we come today.

For his long fruitful life, for the influence of his witness, and for the heritage which is now his according to Thy promise—we express our gratitude.

O Lord, we pray that each of our lives may be strengthened by the inspiration of his life, even to the end of our days. As our Lord has shown us the blessedness of heaven on earth and has called us into the kingdom out of this world, so may our life be deepened in those things which do not pass away.

In trust we commit our loved one to Thy loving and eternal care, knowing it to be more blessed than anything we have experienced and more glorious than we can desire or pray for. In confidence we will wait until our earthly pilgrimage is ended, then reach for our everlasting home in that place not made by man, through Jesus Christ and His Resurrection. *Amen.*

Meditation   "The Resurrected Body"

The Apostle Paul, great mind that he was, spoke to the questions which haunt our minds at the time of death. What will the future be like? If there is resurrection, what kind of body will we have?

In an attempt to describe the essentially indescribable and to express the inexpressible, Paul uses the analogy of a seed.

The seed is put into the ground and dies, but ultimately it rises with a very different kind of body from that with which it was sown. Paul shows that, at one and the same time, there can be dissolution, difference, and yet continuity. The seed is dissolved; when it rises there is a vast difference in the body God gave it; yet in spite of difference, it is the same life, the same seed. Our earthly bodies will be buried and will dissolve. They will rise in a different form, but it is the same person who rises. Your loved one may be dissolved by death; he will be changed by resurrection into a glorified spiritual body; but it is still your loved one who continues.

Paul asserts from this analogy that there is not just one kind of body. Each separate part of creation has its own body. The acorn is resurrected into an oak tree, never into a spruce. Wheat seed produces a wheat stalk and wheat grain, never rye. Corn produces corn. The tulip bulb always becomes a tulip. There is an identification and continuity in nature, with each seed having its peculiar resurrected stalk and blossom. So God gives to each of us human creatures a body that is ours. It is reasonable to expect a suitable, recognizable body for the resurrected life.

In life, from here to eternity, is a continuous development—from seed, to stalk, to blossom in plant life. In the human plane, Adam was made from the dust of the earth. But Jesus, the second Adam, is far more than just a man, and incarnates the very Spirit of God Himself. In earth, we have been one with Adam inheriting his death and having his body. In the new life, we are one with Jesus Christ—therefore we share His life and being in a spiritual body.

"We are God's children now; it does not yet appear what we shall be, but we know that when he appears, we shall be like him" (1 John 3:2).

Poem (*optional*)

Seeds

We drop a seed into the ground,
    A tiny, shapeless thing, shriveled and dry,
And, in the fulness of its time, is seen
    A form of peerless beauty, robed and crowned

Beyond the pride of any earthly queen,
   Instinct with loveliness, and sweet and rare,
The perfect emblem of its Maker's care.
This from a shriveled seed?
   —Then may man hope indeed!
For man is but the seed of what he shall be,
   When, in the fulness of his perfecting,
He drops the husk and cleaves his upward way,
   Through earth's retardings and the clinging clay,
Into the sunshine of God's perfect day.
   No fetters then! No bonds of time or space!
But powers as ample as the boundless grace
   That suffered man, and death, and yet in tenderness,
Set wide the door, and passed Himself before—
   As He had promised—to prepare a place.
We know not what we shall be—only this—

That we shall be made like Him—as He is.[42]

Hymn (*optional*)   "Look, Ye Saints! The Sight Is Glorious" (*solo, song by congregation, organ interlude, or reading by minister*)

Benediction   The God of all grace, who calls you to share his eternal glory in union with Christ, will himself perfect you, and give you firmness, strength, and a sure foundation. To him be the power for ever! Amen (1 Peter 5:10, 11).

Postlude   "Christ the Lord Is Risen Today"; "Thine Is the Glory"

Let him return to the Lord, that he may have mercy on him.

23

FOR AN UNCHURCHED PERSON

Instrumental Prelude　"God So Loved the World" (Stainer); "O God, Have Mercy" (Bach)

The Opening Sentences　Seek the LORD while he may be found, call upon him while he is near; let the wicked forsake his way, and the unrighteous man his thoughts; let him return to the LORD, that he may have mercy on him, and to our God, for he will abundantly pardon (Isaiah 55:6, 7).

Invocation Prayer　O Thou who art the author of our being, the One whose thought designed our existence, whose purposes were seen in Jesus of Nazareth; and who has awakened in us a positive response to truth and love—we bow in reverent humility and thanksgiving.

Deep within us, O God, is a sense of incompleteness. Within us we have aspirations that can never be satisfied in this world.

Grant that we may see in death and in Thy mysterious future, the opportunity for life's fulfillment and completed purposes, as in Jesus Christ. *Amen.*

Scripture Readings

From the Old Testament I waited patiently for the LORD; he inclined to me and heard my cry. He drew me up from the desolate pit, out of the miry bog, and set my feet upon a rock, making my steps secure. He put a new song in my mouth, a song of praise to our God. Many will see and fear, and put their trust in the LORD.

Blessed is the man who makes the LORD his trust, who does not turn to the proud, to those who go astray after false gods! Thou has multiplied, O LORD my God, thy wondrous deeds and thy thoughts toward us; none can compare with thee! Were I to proclaim and tell of them, they would be more than can be numbered . . . Do not thou, O LORD, withhold thy mercy from me, let thy steadfast love and thy faithfulness ever preserve me! For evils have encompassed me without number; my iniquities have overtaken me, till I cannot see; they are more than the hairs of my head; my heart fails me. Be pleased, O LORD, to deliver me! O LORD, make haste to help me! . . . But may all who seek thee rejoice and be glad in thee; may those who love thy salvation say continually, "Great is the LORD!" (Psalms 40:1–5, 11–13, 16).

From the New Testament One of the criminals hanging there threw insults at him: "Aren't you the Messiah? Save yourself and us!" The other one, however, rebuked him, saying: "Don't you fear God? Here we are all under the same sentence. Ours, however, is only right, for we are getting what we deserve for what we did; but he has done no wrong." And he said to Jesus, "Remember me, Jesus, when you come as King!" Jesus said to him, "I tell you this: today you will be in Paradise with me" (Luke 23:39–43).

Finally, build up your strength in union with the Lord, and by means of his mighty power. Put on all the armor that God gives you, so that you will stand up against the Devil's evil tricks. For we are not fighting against human beings, but against the wicked spiritual forces in the heavenly world, the rulers, authorities, and cosmic powers of this dark age. So take up God's armor now! Then when the evil day comes, you will be able to resist the enemy's attacks, and after fighting to the end, you will still hold your ground.

So stand ready: have truth for a belt tight around your waist; put on righteousness for your breastplate, and the readiness to announce the Good News of peace as shoes for your feet. At all times carry faith as a shield; with it you will be able to put out all the burning arrows shot by the Evil One. And accept salvation for a helmet, and the word of God as the sword that the Spirit gives you. Do all this in prayer, asking for God's help. Pray on every occasion, as the Spirit leads (Ephesians 6:10–18a).

Poems (*optional*)

> So I go on, not knowing,
>   —I would not, if I might—
> I would rather walk in the dark with God
>   Than go alone in the light;
> I would rather walk with him by faith
>   Than walk alone by sight.[43]

A Plan Far Greater

There is a plan far greater than the plan you know,
　There is a landscape broader than the one you see.
There is a haven where storm-tossed souls may go—
　You call it death—we, immortality.

You call it death—this seeming endless sleep,
　We call it birth—the soul at last set free.
'Tis hampered not by time or space—you weep.
　Why weep at death? 'Tis immortality.

Farewell, dear voyageur—'twill not be long.
　Thy work is done—now may peace rest with thee.
The kindly thoughts and deeds—they will live on.
　This is not death—'tis immortality.

Farewell, dear voyageur—the river winds and turns,
　The cadence of thy song wafts near to me,
And now thou know'st the thing that all men learn;
　There is no death—there's immortality.[44]

If We Could See Beyond Today

If we could see beyond today
　As God can see,
If all the clouds should roll away,
　The shadows flee;
O'er present griefs we would not fret,
Each sorrow we would soon forget,
For many joys are waiting yet
　For you and me.

If we could know beyond today
　As God doth know,
Why dearest treasures pass away,
　And tears must flow;

And why the darkness leads to light,
Why dreary days will soon grow bright,
Some day life's wrong will be made right,
　　Faith tells us so.

If we could see, if we could know
　　We often say,
But God in love a veil doth throw
　　Across our way.
We cannot see what lies before,
And so we cling to Him the more,
He leads us till this life is o'er,
　　Trust and obey.[45]

Hymn (*optional*)   "Dear Lord and Father of Mankind" (*solo, song by congregation, organ interlude, or reading by minister*)

Meditation   "Sensing the Invisible"

This is a great secret for anyone up against life's distresses. What we need most of all when facing the experience of death, is not a strong constitution, or an imperturbable temperament, nor stoic psychology of detachment. What we need above all else is a sense of the unseen, a consciousness that beyond this visible environment is an invisible realm. The person who can stand fast, though the world crushes in about him, is that one who has a vision of the living Christ, who has entered into a union with Him, and who is confident in this faith. The unseen things of life are every bit as real as the things we see. The only interpretation of life that makes sense of the universe is in the terms of the unseen. We could not live a minute merely on the basis of what we can see or prove. We are strong and confident when we walk by faith in the unseen realities. "He endures, as seeing Him who is invisible."

As you, dear friends, face the loss and adjustment of this death, do not fear. As you face your own dying, which inevitably comes to each, do not be afraid. "The LORD is my light and my salvation; whom shall I fear? the LORD is the stronghold of my life; of whom shall I be afraid?" (Psalms 27:1, 2). Such faith will dispel fear.

The Book of Acts records the dying of a young brave martyr. His name was Stephen, who because he preached the Gospel, was stoned by the inflamed, fanatic, radical Pharisees among whom was Saul of Tarsus. "Death to the heretics," they shouted. "Beat the life out of him. Silence him forever!" Under the whirling torrent of man's inhumanity, Stephen was knocked to his knees; his head was beaten to a pulp; blood was streaming into his eyes; his end was near. Suddenly, for one moment he gazed up, his disfigured face was lifted, and a strange cry from his bleeding lips echoed and re-echoes down through the centuries. "Behold, I see the heavens opened, and the Son of man standing at the right hand of God . . . Lord Jesus, receive my spirit" (Acts 7:56, 59). Then he died, but as the Hebrew author said, "He endured, as seeing Him who is invisible."

How often we have heard from those hanging between life and death, in their semi-conscious state, the testimony about the beautiful realm, descriptions of a vision of heaven, the image of saints in the great cloud of witnesses. "Jesus, lover of my soul, let me to Thy bosom fly."

Remember John Bunyan's vision in *Pilgrim's Prog-*

ress? Mr. Valiant-for-Truth is summoned to cross the final river. As he goes he asks, "Death, where is thy sting?" As he goes further, "Grave, where is thy victory?" As he passes over, nearing another shore, trumpets sound for him from the other side!

> O world invisible, we view thee,
> O world intangible, we touch thee,
> O world unknowable, we know thee,
> Inapprehensible, we clutch thee.[46]

He endures who sees Him who is invisible.

Benediction   O God, grant us the vision of the invisible, that in the face of death, we shall see Thee face-to-face, thus rejoice in Thy presence and find courage and peace forevermore. *Amen.*

Postlude   "Love Divine, All Love Excelling"; "Jesus, Lover of My Soul"

> *Blessed is the man who makes the* Lord *his trust.*

24

FOR A PERSON
OF ANOTHER RELIGION

Instrumental Prelude   "Adagio" (Schumann); "Hark! A Voice Saith, All Is Mortal" (J. S. Bach)

The Opening Sentences   Our help is in the name of the LORD, who made heaven and earth (Psalms 124:8). The eternal God is your dwelling place, and underneath are the everlasting arms (Deuteronomy 33:27).

Invocation Prayer   God and Father of all mankind, who are known by the pure in heart; from whom we have all come; we thank Thee for the gift of life; for its wonder and mystery, its interests and joys, its friendships and relationships. We thank Thee for the ties that bind us to one another. We sorrow that death has invaded our circles of family and fellowship. At the end of human knowledge and help, we can but turn to Thee, unto whom we all must return, whose mercy never fails, and whose name is ever holy. *Amen.*

Scripture Readings
From the Old Testament (Scriptures of the Jewish and Christian Faiths)   As a hart longs for flowing streams, so longs my soul for thee, O God. My soul thirsts for God, for the living God. When shall I come and behold the face of God? (Psalms 42:1, 2).

I waited patiently for the LORD; he inclined to me and heard my cry. He drew me up from the desolate pit, out of the miry bog, and set my feet upon a rock, making my steps secure. He put a new song in my mouth, a song of praise to our God. Many will see and fear, and put their trust in the LORD.

Blessed is the man who makes the LORD his trust, who does not turn to the proud, to those who go astray after false gods! Thou has multiplied, O LORD my God, thy wondrous deeds and thy thoughts toward us; none can compare with thee! Were I to proclaim and tell of them, they would be more than can be numbered. . . . Do not thou, O LORD, withhold thy mercy from me, let thy steadfast love and thy faithfulness ever preserve me! (Psalms 40:1–5, 11).

From the New Testament (Scriptures of the Christian Faith)   "This is why I tell you: do not be worried about the food and drink you need to stay alive, or about clothes for your body. After all, isn't life worth more than food? And isn't the body worth more than clothes? Look at the birds flying around: they do not plant seeds, gather a harvest, and put it in barns; your Father in heaven takes care of them! Aren't you worth much more than birds? Which one of you can live a few years more by worrying about it?

"And why worry about clothes? Look how the wild flowers grow: they do not work or make clothes for themselves. But I tell you that not even Solomon, as rich as he was, had clothes as beautiful as one of these flowers. It is God who clothes the wild grass—grass that is here today, gone tomorrow, burned up in the oven. Will he not be all the more sure to clothe you? How little is your faith! So do not start worrying: 'Where will my food come from? or my drink? or my clothes?' (These are the things the heathen are always after.) Your Father in heaven knows that you need all these things. Instead, give first place to his Kingdom and to what he requires, and he will provide you with all these other things. So do not worry about tomorrow; it will have enough worries of its own. There is no need to add to the troubles each day brings" (Matthew 6:25–34).

Pastoral Prayer   We give thanks, Eternal Spirit, for this friend, recalling before Thee all in him that caused others to love him. We are grateful for all good and gracious influences in his home and work, for all the examples of his devoted, unselfish service. We are thankful for all goodness that has passed from his life into the lives of others, and has made the world better for his presence.

O God, unto whom we all are finally accountable, we leave the future of our brother in Thy providential care, trusting in Thy love and mercy, Thy wisdom and justice. Hear our prayer made in Thy holy name. *Amen.*

Hymn (*optional*)   "Sunset and Evening Star" (*solo or reading by minister*)

Meditation   "Exiting with Trust—Dying with Dignity"

The author-professor, Dr. Reuel Howe, has written a book titled *How to Stay Younger While Growing Older.* He begins the last chapter indicating that frequently when he leads a worship service, just before the benediction, he asks the people to turn and look at the back door of the sanctuary. Soon each will pass through the door to their homes. "Think to yourself," he suggests. "Is that door a door of entrance or of exit?" The answer each person gives to himself makes a difference. "If the answer is *exit* then there is no future. They will leave behind them whatever meaning the worship had for them. If the answer is *entrance* then they are taking the meaning of the worship experience with them and entering with trust into the world outside."

Look at death. Is it an exit door, or an entrance door? To be sure, it is both. At times, death is a welcome exit, an escape from the intolerabilities of life. At other times, death seems like a door of entrance through which we pass to a new stage in life's pilgrimage.

If we can recognize dying as an accompanying experience to living, then acceptance of loss and bereavement can be assimilated meaningfully. Without a proper attitude toward death, we cannot have a proper perspective or love of life.

There is much talk these days about "dying with dignity," with protests against life-prolonging equipment and medicines that keep people alive as mere vegetables. The real secret to "dying with dignity" depends upon the spirit with which we approach death and life. When we have lived well, we may die well. Death gathers up the real things—the cherished thoughts, the precious memories, the victories, the joys, what has given substance and quality to life—and takes these to the door leading to the beyond. It is not the end; it is the beginning. It is exit—but more—it is *entrance*.

We gather here today, and reach back to collect the best things from our friend's life. We see a whole new value to the spiritual dimension. Faith and love seem to grow in our hearts in the very face of his death. All of us drawn around our friend today find sources of refreshments. We are filled with thanksgiving and peace, rather than despair and regret. This death is a fulfillment rather than an emptiness, a gain rather than a loss, a victory rather than a defeat. That is why an ancient prophet said, "It shall come to pass that at evening time there shall be light" (*see* Zechariah 14:7).

Poem (*optional*)

> It singeth low in every heart,
>   We hear it, each and all,—
> A song of those who answer not,
>   However we may call:
> They throng the silence of the breast,
>   We see them as of yore,—
> The kind, the brave, the true, the sweet,
>   Who walk with us no more.
>
> 'Tis hard to take the burden up,
>   When these have laid it down;
> They brightened all the joy of life,
>   They softened every frown;
> But O 'tis good to think of them,
>   When we are troubled sore!
> Thanks be to God that such have been,
>   Though they are here no more.
>
> More homelike seems the vast unknown,
>   Since they have entered there;
> To follow them were not so hard,
>   Wherever they may fare;
> They cannot be where God is not,
>   On any sea or shore;
> Whate'er betides, Thy love abides,
>   Our God, forevermore.[47]

Benediction

"Now, Lord, you have kept your promise,
And you may let your servant go in peace.
For with my own eyes I have seen your salvation,
Which you have made ready in the presence of all peoples:
A light to reveal your way . . .
And to give glory to your people . . ."

(Luke 2:29–32).

May God, the source of hope, fill you with all joy and peace by means of your faith in him, so that your hope will continue to grow by the power of the Holy Spirit (Romans 15:13).

Postlude   "O God, Thou Faithful God" (Karg-Elert)

Thy will be done.

25

FOR A DIFFICULT OCCASION

Instrumental Prelude   "Adagio (*A* Flat)" (Mendelssohn); "Come Thou Fount of Every Blessing"; "I Look to Thee in Every Need"

Meditation   "A Time to Pray"

In such a time of shock and utter despair we are driven to our knees to pray. There is no one to whom we can turn but to God, the "Alpha and Omega" of all creation. Prayer is a common, though mysterious religious exercise. The psalmist affirmed the availability of God, "The Lord is near to all who call upon him . . ." (Psalms 145:18). "Cast your burden upon the Lord and he shall sustain you" (55:22). Jesus said to His disciples, "Ask, and it will be given you; seek, and you will find; knock, and it will be opened to you" (Matthew 7:7).

No doubt, in the past few days, most of you have prayed to God, even when you did not realize it.

There are many meaningful and appropriate prayers in the Bible. None is better known than the one our Lord taught as a model of proper prayer attitudes, suitable content, and appropriate petitions. It is an excellent prayer to pray on this day of bereavement and sorrow.

Our Father who art in heaven. God is the beginner of all existence; the source of our spiritual nature; the Father of our Lord Jesus Christ. He is "ours," all of ours. He is not the sole possession of any one or group. He has a father's warm love for all His children.

Hallowed be Thy name. We reverence God, and respect His mysterious greatness. We praise and glorify Him, not by flippant, coarse words that convey no love or affection. We approach God in humility with a reverent, respectful attitude.

Thy kingdom come. The word *kingdom* refers to the reign of God, the kingdom where grace, love, and righteousness prevail. It is the kingdom of peace and glory. Let that kingdom come! With fervent hearts we yearn for it.

Thy will be done on earth as it is in heaven. This composes our life purpose on earth—to do God's will. This is a difficult prayer; only Jesus could pray it perfectly. Devotion to it caused Him to sweat blood, to stand up against tyrannical forces, and ultimately to lay down His life.

Give us this day our daily bread. Not for tomorrow do we pray. For this day's needs we ask for physical and spiritual strength, trusting the future to the kind providence of God.

Forgive us our sins, as we forgive those who sin against us. All have sinned and missed the mark of God's perfection. We stand in need of His forgiveness if we would escape damnation and achieve heaven's reward. We are forgiven of God in ratio to our willingness to forgive those who misuse and abuse us. Why should we withhold mercy when God has shown mercy toward us? He assures us forgiveness through Jesus Christ, who forgave even those who put Him to death.

Lead us not into temptation but deliver us from evil. We have a breaking point, for we are weak mortals. Keep us from the temptations and tribulations that try our weaknesses, and give us the strength of resistance, so that finally we may be delivered from the corruption and wickedness of this present world. From this vale of tears, grant us a gracious entrance into the abode of eternal joy where "tears shall be wiped away," and pain and death shall be no more.

For Thine is the kingdom and the power and the glory forever. To God belongs all that is good, great, and worthy. To Him belongs all the renown, praise, and adulation. Everything that comes into our lives should serve to praise and glorify God, the King of kings and Lord of lords.

Amen. Yes. Let it be.

Now join your voices and unite your thoughts as we offer to God our Lord's model Prayer:

Our Father who art in heaven, Hallowed be thy name. Thy kingdom come, Thy will be done, On earth as it is in heaven. Give us this day our daily bread. And forgive us our debts, As we forgive our debtors; And lead us not into temptation, But deliver us from evil. For Thine is the kingdom, and the power, and the glory forever. *Amen.*

Benediction   May the words of our mouths and the meditations of our hearts be acceptable in Thy sight, O Lord, our strength and our Redeemer. "May God the Father and Christ Jesus our Lord give you grace, mercy, and peace" (1 Timothy 1:2).

Postlude   "How Great Thou Art"; "Blessed Assurance"

"I am not really alone because the Father is with me."

26

FOR A PERSON WITH NO KNOWN RELATIVES

Instrumental Prelude   "Peace, Perfect Peace"; "Hark, Hark, My Soul"

The Opening Sentences   Wait for the Lord, be strong, and let your heart take courage; yea, wait for the Lord (Psalms 27:14).

Invocation Prayer   O God of peace, who has taught that in quietness and confidence we shall find peace, by

the might of Thy Spirit, lift us into Thy presence, that
we may be still and know that Thou art God, through
Jesus Christ our Lord. *Amen.*

Scripture Readings

From the Old Testament   Lord, thou hast been our
dwelling place in all generations. Before the mountains
were brought forth, or ever thou hadst formed the
earth and the world, from everlasting to everlasting
thou art God . . . . For a thousand years in thy sight.
are but as yesterday when it is past, or as a watch in
the night. Thou dost sweep men away; they are like a
dream, like grass which is renewed in the morning: in
the morning it flourishes and is renewed; in the evening
it fades and withers . . . . The years of our life are
threescore and ten, or even by reason of strength fourscore; yet their span is but toil and trouble; they are
soon gone, and we fly away . . . . So teach us to
number our days that we may get a heart of wisdom . . . . Satisfy us in the morning with thy steadfast love, that we may rejoice and be glad all our
days . . . . Let thy work be manifest to thy servants,
and thy glorious power to their children. Let the favor
of the Lord our God be upon us, and establish thou
the work of our hands upon us, yea, the work of our
hands establish thou it (Psalms 90:1–17).

LORD, let me know my end, and what is the measure
of my days; let me know how fleeting my life is! Behold, thou hast made my days a few handbreadths, and
my lifetime is as nothing in thy sight. Surely every man
stands as a mere breath! . . . And now, Lord, for
what do I wait? My hope is in thee. Deliver me from

all my transgressions. Make me not the scorn of the fool! . . . Hear my prayer, O LORD, and give ear to my cry; hold not thy peace at my tears! For I am thy passing guest, a sojourner, like all my fathers (Psalms 39:4–12).

But truly, as the LORD lives and as your soul lives, there is but a step between me and death (1 Samuel 20:3c).

From the New Testament Jesus answered them: "Do you believe now? The time is coming, and is already here, when all of you will be scattered, each one to his own home, and I will be left all alone. But I am not really alone, because the Father is with me. I have told you this so that you will have peace through your union with me. The world will make you suffer. But be brave! I have defeated the world!" (John 16:31–33).

For this reason, then, I fall on my knees before the Father, from whom every family in heaven and on earth receives its true name. I ask God, from the wealth of his glory, to give you power through his Spirit to be strong in your inner selves, and that Christ will make his home in your hearts, through faith. I pray that you may have your roots and foundations in love, and that you, together with all God's people, may have the power to understand how broad and long and high and deep is Christ's love. Yes, may you come to know his love—although it can never be fully known—and so be completely filled with the perfect fulness of God.

To him who is able to do so much more than we can ever ask for, or even think of, by means of the power working in us: to God be the glory in the church and in Christ Jesus, for all time, for ever and ever! Amen (Ephesians 3:14–21).

Poems (*optional*)

Death Is Only an Old Door

Death is only an old door
   Set in a garden wall;
     On quiet hinges it gives, at dusk
     When the thrushes call.

Along the lintel are green leaves,
   Beyond, the light lies still;
     Very weary and willing feet
     Go over that sill.

There is nothing to trouble any heart;
   Nothing to hurt at all.
     Death is only an old door
     In a garden wall.[48]

Pastoral Prayer Lord God, the source of life, and the destiny of our pilgrimage, age after age the faithful saints have trusted in Thee and found that of Thy mercy there is no end. Of Thy providence we have received; now to Thy keeping we return our beloved friend.

Thou alone has understood the loneliness of our neighbor, left without kin but not without friends. Thou hast been his companion through the day and through the night, on the mountain peak and in the valley, in health and through sickness. We cherish his memory and commend his faith.

Gracious loving Father, we are mindful of the joy of reunited kindred spirits and of Thy promise that love never loses its own. Give us once more the assurance of that "spirit-world," transcending the barriers which separate us from Thee and from one another. In this hour may we know that Thou art the God of life, both in this present world and that which is beyond death; so that whatever may befall us, we will be secure in Thy grace and acquaintance. Then may death merely be a stepping over the river to beautiful tomorrows, through Jesus Christ and His Resurrection. *Amen.*

Hymn (*optional*) "Sunset and Evening Star" (also found in some sources as "Crossing the Bar")—(*solo, song by congregation, organ interlude, or reading by minister*)

Meditation "The Great Reunion"

The question "Which is the happiest season of life?" was referred to an aged man. He replied: "When spring comes, and in the soft air the buds are breaking on the trees, and they are covered with blossoms, I think, 'How beautiful is spring!' Then when the summer comes, and covers the trees with its heavy foliage, and singing birds are among the branches, I think, 'How beautiful is summer!' When autumn loads them with golden fruit, and their leaves bear the gorgeous tint of frost, I think, 'How beautiful is autumn!' But when it is winter, and there is neither foliage nor fruit, then I look up through the leafless branches, as I never could until now, and see the stars shine. That is the happiest season of all." [49]

Seldom does it happen, but occasionally someone outlives all of his family, all of his close friends, and most of his contemporaries. Life becomes lonely, isolated, fear-ridden. To our best knowledge, such is the case with _____. His family—wife, children, brothers and sisters—all have predeceased him. His closest friends have taken the journey to the unknown. He has befriended all of them in their final rites; ironically he has been left alone. We are here to do for him what he has done for others.

For years, he has been ready for the reunion. Now it has come. Death is the door that opens to the Father's house.

Much has been written in recent years about people on the verge of death, then revived to describe the experience. *To Live Again* by Catherine Marshall, *Life After Life* by Raymond A. Moody, Jr., and *On Death and Dying* by Dr. Elizabeth Kubler-Ross are only a few among many. Unanimously the testimony is that death is nothing to fear, that the future is beautiful, solid, and joyful. Many did not want to return to earthly life, for death meant a reunion for which they yearned. They could see images of loved ones gone before.

If we could glimpse into the eternity God has prepared for His faithful, and see the stars shine, we would not call our loved ones back to the drab loneliness of this world.

Some months ago we sent by air freight to our daughter 1,200 miles away the cutest little white and black border collie puppy you could imagine. Her name was Missy. I prepared a small comfortable kennel with padding, food, and water—then took the dog to the air terminal for the long wait. Missy shook with fright of the unknown. The loud noises unnerved her. In every way she could she whined and begged not to go. With a keen love for dogs—especially this one—I was grieved and sick at heart to see her endure the ordeal. I almost didn't let her go. I waved to her as she was taken, and, I confess, tears dampened my cheeks.

That experience is somewhat like death. We hold on to our loved ones, as long as possible. It is a painful journey for all concerned—fear, regret, sorrow, doubt beset us. Inevitably death snatches those we love and they are taken.

As our Missy's flight ended, my daughter eagerly awaited her arrival. Oh, what a glad reunion it was. Missy jumped and licked, smiled and vocalized with joy. She found a new home where she was loved and cared for, even better than we had provided.

How much more is that reunion of loved ones in God's heaven. Will Rogers felt something like this when he wrote a foreword to the book *Trails Plowed Under* by his friend Charles Russell, who died before the book was published. In his "Letter to Charley," Will said in characteristic cowboy language:

You know the Big Boss gent sent a hand over and got you so quick, Charley, but I guess He needed a good man pretty bad. I knew they had been a-working shorthanded over there pretty much all the time. I guess it's hard for Him to get hold of good men; they are just getting scarce everywhere . . . . I bet you hadn't been up there three days, Charley, until you had out your pencil and was a-drawin' something funny. And I bet you that Mark Twain, and old Bill Nye, and Whitcomb Riley, and a whole bunch of those old joshers was just a-waitin' for you to pop in with all the latest ones. And I bet they are regular fellows when you meet 'em, ain't they? Most big men are . . . . When I get to thinking about all them

Top Hands up there, if I could just hold a horse wrangling job with 'em, I wouldn't mind following that wagon myself. Well, you will run onto my old Dad up there, Charley, for he was a real cowhand, and I bet he is runnin' a wagon; and you will pop into some well-kept ranch house, over under cool shady trees, and you will be asked to have dinner, and it will be the best one you ever had in your life. Well, when you are thankin' the women folks you just tell the sweet lookin' little old lady that you knew her boy back on an outfit you used to rope for, and tell the daughters that you knew their brother, and if you see a cute little rascal runnin' round there with my brand on him, kiss him for me. Well, can't write any more, Charley, paper's all wet. It must be raining in this old bunkhouse. Of course, we're all just hangin' on here as long as we can. I don't know why we hate to go, we know it's better there. From your old friend, Will.[50]

Benediction   May all our days be lived unto Thee, merciful God, until the last morning breaks, and the shadows flee away; then in Thy mercy, unite us with all whom we have loved, in the name of Jesus Christ, our risen Lord. *Amen.*

Postlude   "Largo"; "Ten Thousand Times Ten Thousand"

"Be brave! I have defeated the world."

27

FOR GENERAL USE

Instrumental Prelude "Nearer My God to Thee"; "All Creatures of Our God and King"

The Opening Sentences "Come to me, all of you who are tired from carrying your heavy loads, and I will give you rest. Take my yoke and put it on you, and learn from me, for I am gentle and humble in spirit; and you will find rest. The yoke I will give you is easy, and the load I will put on you is light" (Matthew 11:28–30).

Invocation Prayer Almighty God, our Father, from whom we come, and to whom our spirits return; thou hast been our dwelling place in all generations. Thou art our refuge and strength; a very present help in trouble. Grant us thy leading in this hour, and enable us to put our trust in thee, that the memory of a life well lived, that the confidence of an eternal triumph achieved, may calm our spirits and comfort our hearts. Lift our eyes beyond the shadows of the earth to see in the light of life immortal. So may we find grace and strength for this and every time of need; through Jesus Christ our Lord. *Amen.*[51]

It's dark now—
And I'm flying low,
Cold.
But deep within me
I remember
A darkness like this
That came before.

And I remember
That after that hard dark
That long dark—
Dawn broke.
And the sun rose again.

And that is what I must
Remember now.[52]

". . . I will be left all alone. But I am not really alone, because the Father is with me. I have told you this so that you will have peace through your union with me. The world will make you suffer. But be brave! I have defeated the world!" (John 16:32, 33).

"I will ask the Father, and he will give you another Helper, the Spirit of truth, to stay with you forever. The world cannot receive him, because it cannot see him or know him. But you know him, for he remains with you and lives in you. I will not leave you alone; I will come back to you" (John 14:16–18).

"I have told you this while I am still with you. The Helper, the Holy Spirit whom the Father will send in my name, will teach you everything, and make you remember all that I have told you. Peace I leave with you; my own peace I give you. I do not give it to you as the world does. Do not be worried and upset; do not be afraid" (John 14:25–27).

Whither shall I go from thy Spirit? Or whither shall I flee from thy presence? If I ascend to heaven, thou art there! If I make my bed in Sheol, thou art there! If I take the wings of the morning and dwell in the uttermost parts of the sea, even there thy hand shall lead me, and thy right hand shall hold me. If I say, "Let only darkness cover me, and the light about me be night," even the darkness is not dark to thee, the night is bright as the day; the darkness is as light with thee (Psalms 139:7–12).

Hymn (*optional*) "Great Is Thy Faithfulness" (*solo or reading by minister*)

Bless the LORD, O my soul; and all that is within me, bless his holy name! Bless the LORD, O my soul, and forget not all his benefits, who forgives all your iniquity, who heals all your diseases, who redeems your life from the Pit, who crowns you with steadfast love and mercy (Psalms 103:1–4).

The LORD is my shepherd, I shall not want; he makes me lie down in green pastures. He leads me beside still waters, he restores my soul. He leads me in paths of righteousness for his name's sake.

Even though I walk through the valley of the shadow of death, I fear no evil; for thou art with me; thy rod and thy staff, they comfort me.

Thou preparest a table before me in the presence of my enemies; thou anointest my head with oil, my cup overflows. Surely goodness and mercy shall follow me

all the days of my life; and I shall dwell in the house
of the Lord for ever (Psalm 23).

The Weaver

My life is but a weaving
  Between my Lord and me;
I may not choose the colors,
  He knows what they should be;
For He can view the pattern
  Upon the upper side,
While I can see it only
  On this, the under side.

Sometimes He weaveth sorrow,
  Which seemeth strange to me;
But I will trust His judgment,
  And work on faithfully;
'Tis He who fills the shuttle,
  He knows just what is best,
So I shall weave in earnest
  And leave with Him the rest.

Not till the loom is silent
  And the shuttles cease to fly
Shall God unroll the canvas
  And explain the reason why—
The dark threads are as needful
  In the Weaver's skillful hand
As the threads of gold and silver
  In the pattern He has planned.[53]

Hymn (*optional*)   "Back of the Clouds"

"Do not be worried and upset," Jesus told them.
"Believe in God, and believe also in me. There are
many rooms in my Father's house, and I am going to

prepare a place for you. I would not tell you this if it were not so. And after I go and prepare a place for you, I will come back and take you to myself, so that you will be where I am" . . . . Jesus answered him: "I am the way, I am the truth, I am the life; no one goes to the Father except by me" (John 14:1–6).

Jesus said to her: "I am the resurrection and the life. Whoever believes in me will live, even though he dies; and whoever lives and believes in me will never die. Do you believe this?" (John 11:25, 26).

Who, then, can separate us from the love of Christ? Can trouble do it, or hardship, or persecution, or hunger, or poverty, or danger, or death? . . . No, in all these things we have complete victory through him who loved us! For I am certain that nothing can separate us from his love: neither death nor life; neither angels nor other heavenly rulers or powers; neither the present nor the future; neither the world above nor the world below—there is nothing in all creation that will ever be able to separate us from the love of God which is ours through Christ Jesus our Lord (Romans 8:35, 37–39).

Hymn (*optional*)   "Under His Wings" (*solo, song by congregation, organ interlude, or reading by minister*)

The Holy Springtime

The flowers that bloom through the summer,
  In the autumn will be dead;
And all winter long 'neath the cover of snow
  Their beauty will be hid.

But when the bright springtime comes,
  To waken them from their sleep,
Their hidden beauty again will appear,
  Their soft petals again will be sweet.

So it is with the people:
  For when God sees best,
After their summer of ceaseless bloom,
  He will give them a winter's rest.
He will cause the autumn winds
  To make them droop and die;
And we will long for those beautiful flowers,
  As the winter days go by.

But the springtime, too, will come to them,
  And God will waken them all;
O then, how pure and sweet and holy,
  They will bloom to answer His call!
God will be the Gardener,
  In that Great Garden of Flowers,
And all the time of eternity
  Will be filled with bright springtime hours.[54]

The Rose Beyond the Wall

Near a shady wall a rose once grew,
  Budded and blossomed in God's free light,
Watered and fed by morning dew,
  Shedding its sweetness day and night.

As it grew and blossomed fair and tall
  Slowly rising to loftier height,
It came to a crevice in the wall
  Through which there shone a beam of light.

Onward it crept with added strength
  With never a thought of fear or pride,

It followed the light through the crevice's length
    And unfolded itself on the other side.

The light, the dew, the broadening view
    Were found the same as they were before,
And it lost itself in beauties new,
    Breathing its fragrance more and more.

Shall claim of death cause us to grieve
    And make our courage faint and fall,
Nay! Let us faith and hope receive;
    The rose still grows beyond the wall.

Scattering fragrance far and wide,
    Just as it did in days of yore,
Just as it did on the other side,
    Just as it will for evermore.[55]

So live, that when thy summons comes to join
The innumerable caravan, which moves
To that mysterious realm, where each shall take
His chamber in the silent halls of death,
Thou go not, like the quarry-slave at night,
Scourged to his dungeon, but, sustained and soothed
By an unfaltering trust, approach thy grave
Like one who wraps the drapery of his couch
About him, and lies down to pleasant dreams.[56]

Hymn (*optional*)   "God Will Take Care of You"
(*solo, song by congregation, organ interlude, or reading by minister*)

Unison Lord's Prayer   Our Father, who art in heaven, Hallowed be Thy Name. Thy kingdom come, Thy will be done on earth as it is in heaven. Give us this day our daily bread; and forgive us our debts, as we forgive our debtors. And lead us not into temptation, but deliver us from evil; for Thine is the kingdom, and the power, and the glory forever. *Amen.*

Postlude   "The Funeral March" (Chopin); "O Love That Wilt Not Let Me Go"

I shall dwell in the house of the Lord forever.

28

THE SERVICE AT THE GRAVE

Appropriate Scriptures
From the Old Testament (Select one or two.)
  O Lord, our Lord, how majestic is thy name in all the earth! . . . When I look at thy heavens, the work of thy fingers, the moon and the stars which thou hast established; what is man that thou art mindful of him, and the son of man that thou dost care for him? Yet thou hast made him little less than God, and dost crown him with glory and honor (Psalms 8:1, 3–5).

———

  The LORD is my shepherd, I shall not want; he makes me lie down in green pastures. He leads me beside still waters; he restores my soul. He leads me in paths of righteousness for his name's sake. Even though I walk through the valley of the shadow of death, I fear no evil; for thou art with me; thy rod and thy staff, they comfort me.

Thou preparest a table before me in the presence of my enemies; thou anointest my head with oil, my cup overflows. Surely goodness and mercy shall follow me all the days of my life; and I shall dwell in the house of the Lord for ever (Psalm 23).

———

Thou dost guide me with thy counsel, and afterward thou wilt receive me to glory. Whom have I in heaven but thee? And there is nothing upon earth that I desire besides thee. My flesh and my heart may fail, but God is the strength of my heart and my portion for ever (Psalms 73:24–26).

———

I will lift up my eyes to the hills. From whence does my help come? My help comes from the LORD, who made heaven and earth. He will not let your foot be moved, he who keeps you will not slumber. Behold, he who keeps Israel will neither slumber nor sleep (Psalms 121:1–4).

———

For everything there is a season, and a time for every matter under heaven: a time to be born, and a time to die; a time to plant, and a time to pluck up what is planted; . . . a time to weep and a time to laugh; a time to mourn, and a time to dance (Ecclesiastes 3:1–4).

———

From the New Testament (*Select one or two.*)

This is how it will be when the dead are raised to life. When the body is buried it is mortal; when raised, it will be immortal . . . . When buried, it is a physical body; when raised, it will be a spiritual body. There is, of course, a physical body, so there has to be a spiritual body (1 Corinthians 15:42–44).

———

But the truth is that Christ has been raised from death, as the guarantee that those who sleep in death will also be raised. For just as death came by means of a man, in the same way the rising from death comes by means of a man. For just as all men die because of their union to Adam, in the same way all will be raised to life because of their union to Christ (1 Corinthians 15:20–22).

———

This is what I mean, brothers: what is made of flesh and blood cannot share in God's Kingdom, and what is mortal cannot possess immortality.

Listen to this secret: we shall not all die, but in an instant we shall all be changed, as quickly as the blinking of an eye, when the last trumpet sounds. For when it sounds, the dead will be raised immortal beings, and we shall all be changed. For what is mortal must clothe itself with what is immortal; what will die must clothe itself with what cannot die. So when what is mortal has been clothed with what is immortal, and when what will die has been clothed with what cannot die, then the scripture will come true: "Death is destroyed; victory is complete!"

"Where, O Death, is your victory? Where, O Death, is your power to hurt?"

Death gets its power to hurt from sin, and sin gets its

power from the Law. But thanks be to God who gives us the victory through our Lord Jesus Christ!

So then, my dear brothers, stand firm and steady. Keep busy always in your work for the Lord, since you know that nothing you do in the Lord's service is ever without value (1 Corinthians 15:50–58).

———

For this reason we never become discouraged. Even though our physical being is gradually decaying, yet our spiritual being is renewed day after day. And this small and temporary trouble we suffer will bring us a tremendous and eternal glory, much greater than the trouble. For we fix our attention, not on things that are seen, but on things that are unseen. What can be seen lasts only for a time; but what cannot be seen lasts for ever (2 Corinthians 4:16–18).

———

For we know that when this tent we live in—our body here on earth—is torn down, God will have a house in heaven for us to live in, a home he himself made, which will last for ever (2 Corinthians 5:1).

———

Then I heard a voice from heaven saying: "Write this: Happy are the dead who from now on die in the service of the Lord!" "Certainly so," answers the Spirit. "They will enjoy rest from their hard work; for they take with them the results of their service" (Revelation 14:13).

Suitable Poems

> Now, the laborer's task is o'er;
> Now, the battle day is past;

Now upon the farther shore
    Lands the voyager at last.
Father, in Thy gracious keeping
Leave we now Thy servant sleeping.[57]

I know not what the future hath
    Of marvel or surprise,
Assured alone that life and death
    His mercy underlies.[58]

. . . Another day
Shall chase the bitter dark away;
What though our eyes with tears be wet;
The sunrise never faileth us yet.

The blush of dawn may yet restore
Our light and hope and joy once more.
Sad soul, take comfort, nor forget
That sunrise never faileth us yet.[59]

There is no death! The stars go down
    To rise upon some other shore,
And bright in heaven's jeweled crown
    They shine for evermore.

There is no death! the dust we tread
    Shall change, beneath the summer showers
To golden grain, or mellow fruit,
    Or rainbow-tinted flowers.

And ever near us, though unseen,
    The dear immortal spirits tread,
For all the boundless universe
    Is life—there are no dead.[60]

Life is real! Life is earnest!
    And the grave is not its goal;

Dust thou art, to dust returnest,
Was not spoken of the soul.[61]

———

Strong Son of God, immortal Love,
Whom we, that have not seen thy face,
By faith, and faith alone, embrace,
Believing where we cannot prove . . .
Thou wilt not leave us in the dust:
Thou madest man, he knows not why,
He thinks he was not made to die;
And thou hast made him: thou art just.[62]

———

Swing softly, beauteous gates of death,
To let a waiting soul pass on,
Achievement crowns life's purposes
And victory is forever won.

Swing softly, softly, heavenly gate,
Thy portal passed, no more to roam;
Our traveler finds her journey o'er,
And rest at last in "Home Sweet Home." [63]

———

Calm on the bosom of thy God,
Fair spirit, rest thee now!
Even while with ours thy footsteps trod,
His seal was on thy brow.

Dust, to its narrow house beneath!
Soul, to its place on high!
They that have seen thy look in death
No more may fear to die.

Lone are the paths, and sad the bowers,
Whence thy meek smile is gone;
But oh! a brighter home than ours
In heaven, is now thine own.[64]

———

"Goodby, till morning come again,"
We part, if part we must, with pain,
But night is short, and hope is sweet,
Faith fills our hearts, and wings our feet;
And so we sing the old refrain,
"Goodby, till morning come again."

"Goodby, till morning come again,"
The thought of death brings weight of pain.
But could we know how short the night
That falls, and hides them from our sight,
Our hearts would sing the old refrain,
"Goodby, till morning come again." [65]

———

E'en for the dead I will not bind
   My soul to grief—death cannot long divide:
For is it not as if the rose that climbed
   My garden wall had blossomed on the other side?
Death doth hide but not divide;
   Beloved, thou art on Christ's other side. [66]

———

The hope sublime that soared into the sky,
   Can such hope die?
The faith serene that smiled at death,
   Was it but breath?
The love that served and took no thought of cost,
   Can it be lost?
Nay, is it not with forces such as these
   God peoples His eternities? [67]

———

Not for him but for us should our tears be shed,
Mourn, mourn, for the living, but not for the dead.
Let the dirge be unsung, and awaken the psalm,
No cypress for him who lies crowned with the palm. [68]

———

What must it be to step on shore, and find it—Heaven;
To take hold of a hand, and find it—God's hand;

To breathe a new air and find it—Celestial air;
To feel invigorated, and find it—Immortality;
To rise from the care and turmoil of earth
Into one unbroken calm;
To wake up and find it—Glory.[69]

———

> Out of the dusk a shadow,
>   Then a spark;
> Out of the cloud a silence,
>   Then a lark;
> Out of the heart a rapture,
>   Then a pain;
> Out of the dead, cold ashes,
>   Life again.[70]

Committals

For a Child

Now we commit to the care of our Heavenly Father this little child, trusting the compassionate, loving Savior's words, when He took children in His arms and said, "of such is the Kingdom of Heaven." "He shall feed his flock like a shepherd; he shall gather the lambs with his arm, and carry them in his bosom."

Inasmuch as the spirit has departed this little body, we commit his form to the earth, amidst the beautiful flowers and trees of this tranquil garden. But the true child, which is the spirit, we commend to the keeping of the Eternal Father, in whom the spirit has life everlasting, assured in the Resurrection of Jesus Christ, our Lord.

The Committal Prayer O tender Shepherd, carry this little lamb into the green pastures and beside the still waters of Thy paradise, among the happy company of the glorified children. Hold him close to Thy bosom of warmth and love so that there will be nothing to fear. When at last the mystery of Thy providence shall be unveiled to our understanding, restore this child to these yearning hearts, so that these tears of farewell may one day, as Thou hast promised, become the tears of welcome and gladness.

The peace of God, which passes all understanding, keep your hearts and your minds in the knowledge and love of God and His Son, Jesus Christ our Lord. *Amen.*

For a Faithful Christian

For as much as the spirit has departed from the body, we here commit the body to its final resting place in this sacred city of the dead, amid these beautiful trees and flowers, and comrades of earth. But the true spiritual person, who is not confined to flesh and blood, we commend to Almighty God, in whom is life everlasting, according to the Resurrection of Jesus Christ, assured that as we have borne the image of the earthly, so shall we bear the image of the heavenly.

The Committal Prayer We seem to give him back to Thee, dear God, whom You gave to us. Yet, as Thou did not lose him in giving, so we have not lost him by his returning.

O Lord of our souls, what You give, You do not really take away, for what is Yours is ours always, if we are Yours.

Lift us up, strong Son of God, that we may see further; cleanse our eyes that we may see more clearly; and draw us to Thyself that we may know ourselves to be nearer to our beloved who art with Thee. While Thou are preparing a place for us, prepare us for that happy place, that where they are, and where Thou art, we may be, through Jesus Christ. *Amen.*

For General Use

Our hearts still cling to this body, because we cannot disassociate it from the beloved one who dwelt in and animated it; but it is really only the wornout garment which the loved one has cast aside. Hence, while reverencing it because of the tender memories that gather about it, we consign it now to its original element, looking with confidence to the fashioning of that perfect body which is in Christ Jesus.

For an Unchurched Person

Forasmuch as death has invaded our ranks once again, and the soul of our departed has passed into the unknown beyond, we therefore commit his body to its resting place amid these peaceful surroundings, relying on the promised word, "As a father pities his children, so the LORD pities those who fear him" (Psalms 103:13).

For an Aged Person

Forasmuch as the spirit has departed the body, we do commit this body to its final resting place in the earth, as it was in the beginning. But the Spirit, which is the true person, we commit into the care of Almighty God, the Alpha and Omega, in whom is the hope of everlasting life, through Jesus Christ our Lord. *Amen.*

At a Mausoleum

Forasmuch as our friend has come to the end of his earthly journey, we leave his body here in this place prepared for it; and the spirit we commend to God's eternal keeping.

At a Columbarium

Again death has invaded our ranks and taken our brother. We bear his body to this place prepared for it that ashes may return to ashes, and dust to dust, and we commit his spirit to God who gave it, world without end.

General Committal Prayer God, source of life, and our hope in death, in Thy mercy we trust. Here in this place of beauty and memory, may our hearts be receptive to Thee, where eternal rest is to be found. As the changes of life leave us lonelier, grant us to live in the light of death's possibility and eternal life's reality, that we may be quickened in conscience, sensitive to Thy presence and purposes, so to live out our days in Thy love and service until Thy summons calls us from this earthly pilgrimage. In Jesus' name. *Amen.*

Benediction May the God of peace provide you with every good thing you need in order to do his will, and may he, through Jesus Christ, do in us what pleases him. And to Christ be the glory forever and ever. Amen (Hebrews 13:21).

SOURCE NOTES

Chapter 1
1 Henry W. Longfellow.
2 Samuel Hinds.

Chapter 3
3 Mr. and Mrs. Malen Dowse (Scott's parents), Dodge City, Kansas.
4 Used by permission of Charles L. Wallis.

Chapter 4
5 Anonymous.
6 James L. McCreery.
7 Henry Wadsworth Longfellow.

Chapter 5
8 From GLORIOUS DAWN by Charles B. Motley. Copyright, 1947, by C. D. Pantle. Used by permission of The Bethany Press.
9 Philip James Bailey, from "Festus."

Chapter 6
10 Catherine Marshall.

Chapter 7
11 *Sports Illustrated,* September 13, 1976, p. 16.
12 By an anonymous parent.

Chapter 8
13 Helen Steiner Rice.
14 Helen Steiner Rice.
15 John Greenleaf Whittier.

Chapter 9
16 "Sometime" by Mary Riley Smith. Used by permission of Charles L. Wallis.

17   Author unknown.
18   "There Is No Death" by M. E. Dodd. Used by permission of Charles L. Wallis.

Chapter 10
19   Thomas W. Fessenden. Used by permission of Charles L. Wallis.
20   Margaret Sangster.
21   "In My Father's House" by Robert Freeman.

Chapter 11
22   Adapted from *You Can't Go Home Again* by Thomas Wolfe. Used by permission.
23   "Faith" by Ella Wheeler Wilcox.
24   "Some Time We'll Understand" by Maxwell N. Cornelius.

Chapter 12
25   Henry Drummond.

Chapter 14
26   Adapted from THE BOOK OF COMMON ORDER of the Church of Scotland; Oxford University Press, Edinburgh, 1940.

Chapter 15
27   Author unknown.
28   Author unknown.

Chapter 16
29   By Sarah Pratt McClean Green. Used by permission of Charles L. Wallis.

Chapter 17
30   Joaquin Miller.
31   Margaret Widdemer.

Chapter 18
32 Horatius Bonar.
33 Anonymous.

Chapter 20
34 "My Soul Is Bound for Gloryland" by Erwin T. Um-
     bach.
35 "There Is No Death" by M. E. Dodd. Used by per-
     mission of Charles L. Wallis.
36 By John Richard Moreland. Used by permission of
     Charles L. Wallis.
37 James L. Christensen.

Chapter 21
38 By Effa Alexander-Rosenboom from MIDWEST
     CHAPARRAL Magazine, Grand Island, Nebraska,
     Spring 1954 issue. Used by permission.
39 Author unknown.
40 From "A Wayside Altar."
41 By William Cullen Bryant from "Thanatopsis."

Chapter 22
42 By John Oxenham. Used by permission of Miss
     T. Oxenham.

Chapter 23
43 "Be Assured" by Mary Gardner Brainard.
44 Anonymous.
45 By Norman Clayton. Available in tract form from
     Faith, Prayer, & Tract League, Grand Rapids, Mich-
     igan.
46 "In No Strange Land" by Francis Thompson.

Chapter 24
47 "Auld Lang Syne" by John White Chadwick.

Chapter 26
48   Nancy Byrd Turner.
49   Author unknown.
50   From Introduction to *Trails Plowed Under* (New York: Doubleday & Co., Inc., 1927).

Chapter 27
51   G. Edwin Osborn: CHRISTIAN WORSHIP: A SERVICE BOOK; Copyright 1953 by Wilbur H. Cramblet; Christian Board of Publication, St. Louis, Mo.
52   By Ken Walsh, "After the Dark" from *Sometimes I Weep,* The Judson Press. Used by permission.
53   Anonymous.
54   Grace Welker Dowling.
55   A. L. Frink.
56   By William Cullen Bryant from "Thanatopsis."

Chapter 28
57   John Ellerton.
58   From "The Eternal Goodness" by John Greenleaf Whittier.
59   Celia Thaxter.
60   John L. McCreery.
61   From "A Psalm of Life" by Henry Wadsworth Longfellow.
62   From "In Memoriam" by Alfred Lord Tennyson.
63   Alice B. Howe.
64   Felicia Dorothea Hemans.
65   Author unknown.
66   Author unknown.
67   Charles Carroll Albertson.
68   Author unknown.
69   Author unknown.
70   By John B. Tabb from "Evolution."